A New Approach to Literary Theory and Criticism

R.S. Malik
Former Head, Postgraduate Dept. of English,
C.R.A. College, Sonepat (NCR)

Jagdish Batra
Head, English Language Centre
O.P. Jindal Global University, Sonepat (NCR)

ATLANTIC
PUBLISHERS & DISTRIBUTORS (P) LTD

Published by
ATLANTIC
PUBLISHERS & DISTRIBUTORS (P) LTD
7/22, Ansari Road, Darya Ganj, New Delhi-110002
Phones : +91-11-40775252, 23273880, 23275880, 23280451
Fax : +91-11-23285873
Web : www.atlanticbooks.com
E-mail : orders@atlanticbooks.com

Branch Office
5, Nallathambi Street, Wallajah Road, Chennai-600002
Phones : +91-44-64611085, 32413319
E-mail : chennai@atlanticbooks.com

Printed in India at Glorious Printers, A-13, D.S.I.D.C., Jhilmil Industrial Area, Delhi-110095

Preface

The advent of poststructuralism has made literary criticism a highly complex and technical affair, so much so that not only ordinary students but also several teachers feel baffled and bewildered at the prospect of having to deal with it. In order to comprehend literature, one has, in addition to grasping literary theories, to be familiar with numerous linguistic, psychological, political and cultural theories that impact the production and reception of literature these days. From meta-narratives to epistemological premises—all get interrogated in these postmodern times.

This book is not meant to be a comprehensive study of the sprawling domain of critical, literary and cultural theories. It is rather a modest attempt to explain different theories and movements in simple language for the benefit of students of postgraduate classes of Indian universities. The length of the chapters has been kept limited to two to three thousand words each in which the writers have sincerely tried to sum up important concepts and approaches. The format followed in preparing these essays is to begin with the historical development of any theory, elaborate and illustrate different approaches, move on to the key features, critics and methodology, and conclude with its evaluation. An extra edge has been provided through citations from valuable sources relevant to each area of study.

As a matter of record, it may be mentioned that the following chapters have been written by the first author, with the remaining having been dealt with by the second author: New Criticism, Structuralist Criticism, Postmodernism,

American Deconstruction, Marxist Criticism, New Historicism, Gender Studies, Psychoanalytic criticism, Feminist Criticism, Phenomenological Criticism, Reception Theory, Intertextuality, Reader-response Theory, and Social Media Studies.

The book is the result of cumulative endeavour of two professors of literature of long standing, both of whom share the hallowed relationship of teacher and pupil, respectively. Needless to say, their classroom experience of several decades has helped them to prepare concise and compact write-ups which should satisfy the needs of student community. However, there is no limit to improvement; therefore, the authors welcome feedback from students and teachers who are the best judge of the value of this endeavour.

R.S. Malik
Jagdish Batra

Contents

1

Modernism

Although the term 'modern' stands for all that is contemporary or belongs to present, its more restricted meaning in the area of language and literature refers to the phase that began with the beginning of Renaissance in Europe. However, the term 'modernism' has been appropriated for an even more limited use in the domain of culture. It denotes a movement covering all creative arts, especially poetry, fiction, drama, painting, music and architecture beginning around the onset of the twentieth century. Talking about the manifestation of modernism in literature, M.H. Abrams remarks that this term is "widely used to identify new and distinctive features in the subjects, forms, concepts, and styles of literature and other arts in the early decades of the twentieth century, but especially after World War I (1914-18)" (176).

Modernism involves a deliberate and radical **break with tradition** insofar as basis of Western art and culture is concerned. Literary historians place the beginning of the modernist revolt as far back as the 1890s, but the period of high modernism is definitely placed after the start of First World War and before the 1960s, when postmodernism took over. This period was marked by unparalleled changes which occurred rapidly in the form of a series of movements in Europe and America. Some of the leading figures of the movement include Marcel Proust,

Franz Kafka, James Joyce, Ezra Pound, T.S. Eliot, William Faulkner, Virginia Wolf, etc.

The ferocity of violence during the First World War called into question the durability of the Western civilization which had hitherto considered Christianity as a cementing force among the nations. The seemingly sure foundation of the traditional Western art and culture, social organizations and religion, even literary modes and styles seemed suspect. Many scholars in Europe and America attacked the rationalist philosophy. The frustrated modern thinkers found the world chaotic and fragmented. The old ideologies of rationality, science, progress, civilization, imperialism, etc. did not fit into this world. The writers and the artists felt alienated and marginalized. This was a world where language was perceived to be an inadequate instrument for expression and understanding. Thus "Long-held assumptions—the power of reason, the progress of history, providence, the moral autonomy of human beings, the ability of people and nations to live in harmony, as well as our capacity to know ourselves and the world—were plunged into a mode of moral, spiritual and intellectual crisis" (Habib 5).

Philosophically speaking, modernism is the repudiation of a continuity between worlds of subject and object, the self and the world. The human self is now regarded as fluid, flexible and fragmented. There is a perception of the complex roles of time, memory, and history in the mutual construction of self and world. Time is not conceived as static to be separated into past, present and future as discrete elements and in a linear relation. The intellectual roots of modernism are traced to the transcendental idealism of German philosopher Immanuel Kant (1724-1804). In his *Critique of Pure Reason*, he expressed the view that absolute reality cannot be known. Art has, therefore, to be autotelic or having an end in itself. This meant elevating the position of the artist who was now free to act the way he liked and to create his own set of laws. Kant also distinguished between logical discourse that was fit for science and the aesthetic discourse fit for literature. This distinction is fundamental to modernism because modern art is not logical; it is abstract, irrational and surreal.

Schopenhauer's (1788-1860) nihilism and his disciple Nietzsche's (1844-1900) rejection of both reason and conscience as guides to truth and his pronouncement of God being dead influenced modern literature which shows a sense of despair and disillusionment. Sigmund Freud (1856-1939), through his findings in the field of psychology, gave a fillip to the exploration of inner reality in modern art. His discovery of a chaotic unconscious alienated from the conscious mind became an important theme in modern literature.

As it happened with the term 'modernism', the French term **'avant-garde'** also has been delimited. Etymologically, it stands for the 'advance guard' or 'vanguard' in military. By that token, in arts and literature, avant-garde should refer to leaders or pioneers. However, the term is primarily identified with a small group of artists and authors, who went against the themes and forms prevalent in their time at the start of the Modernist phase. They intentionally alienated themselves from the mainstream art and literature and chose to challenge the accepted norms of society. The avant-garde shocked the readers with startling new forms and techniques and bolder subjects. Artistic movements like Cubism, Dadaism, Vorticism, etc. are clubbed under it. Even the French symbolist poets like Verlaine and Mallarme were the first members of the avant-garde. Likewise, the playwrights of the Theatre of the Absurd were counted among the avant-garde. Since counter-movements have always been and shall always be there, therefore, the avant-garde is present even in postmodern times. Over a period of time, the avant-garde espoused the philosophy of 'art for art's sake'.

In English literature, one of the early groups of artists-critics associated with modernism was the **Bloomsbury Group** which included novelists E.M. Forster (1879-1970) and Virginia Woolf (1882-1941), Vanessa Bell (Virginia Woolf's sister), art critics Roger Fry and Clive Bell, economist J.M. Keynes, biographer Lytton Strachey and the painter Duncan Grant. The group exerted influence on the literary and intellectual scene for nearly two decades. The members of the group believed in informal relationships and stressed the importance of pleasure—personal and aesthetic—over other ideals. Their successors also indulged in political activism. In the main, the Bloomsbury Group is known for its criticism of materialistic realism in arts and literature. Clive Bell's insistence on form was shared by others also and was to influence modernistic approach to literature. Pointing to the variety of 'isms', Malcolm Bradbury comments that modernism involves a whole cluster of international movements and tendencies which are "actually often at great variance with one another" (73).

The **literary works** which heralded the modern age are recognized as James Joyce's *Ulysses*, T.S. Eliot's *The Waste Land* and Virginia Woolf's *Jacob's Room*. Many other literary experiments also mark this period. In keeping with the scenario of futility and anarchy, which the contemporary world was, literature too had to dispense with the concepts of order and 'literary' language. Therefore, *The Waste Land* has fragments of utterances and allusions and the reader is hard put to find the connectives between them. This discontinuity of narrative takes the form of stream-of-consciousness in the works of Joyce and Woolf. Inner life becomes more important for these authors than the external world. Techniques like surrealism, impressionism and expressionism were used to advantage. Among the literary figures associated with modernism are Marcel Proust, Franz Kafka, William Carlos Williams, Wallace Stevens, Rainer Maria Rilke, Eugene O'Neil, Bertolt Brecht, etc.

Twentieth century poetry was deeply influenced by **symbolism.** Irish poet and critic W.B. Yeats (1865-1939), the American poet Ezra Pound (1885-1972) and the Anglo-American poet and critic T.S. Eliot (1888-1965) made use of symbolism in their poetry. Some assumptions that form the basis of Eliot's critical notions such as 'tradition', 'dissociation of sensibility' and 'objective correlative' may have had roots in the thoughts of symbolists, especially Remy de Gourmont.

Various modernist groups tended to be **formalistic** in focusing on the formal structure of a work of art. Indeed, literary critics of various historical periods have placed emphasis on the formal aspects of art and literature, but this emphasis scaled new heights in literatures and critical theories of the early twentieth century. It began with the Formalist movement in Russia and Practical Criticism in England. It was during this period that the foundations of New Criticism were laid by such figures as William Empson and I.A. Richards. The latter's *Principles of Literary Criticism* (1924) and *Practical Criticism* (1929) are considered important landmarks. New Criticism treated a literary work as an autonomous and self-contained structure of words only. A detailed description of New Criticism is to be found elsewhere in this book.

Literary modernism was marked by a lot of **complexity and heterogeneity**. We may understand this complexity through an example: the experience of 'love' could be quite different from one person to another. The feeling depends on relationships between friends, spouses, parents, colleagues and so on and the connotation of the expression love changes with the change of context. At times, one might find the signifier 'love' lacking in conveying the feeling in the perfect sense when the persons involved do not ascribe to love as it is known to exist in the categories pointed out here. It is not difficult to comprehend the deficiency of language to express love between two beings. Therefore, modernist poetry, instead of making use of plain language in an overt statement, relies far more on suggestion and allusion. The definitions of reality became increasingly complex. Modernists came to this common awareness by different paths. W.B. Yeats drew on the occult, Irish myths and legends as well as the Romantics and the French Symbolists. Proust drew on the insights of the philosophy of Bergson; Virginia Woolf drew on Bergson. Similarly, Ezra Pound drew on various non-European literatures as well as French writers, and T.S. Eliot on Dante, the Metaphysical poets, Laforgue, Baudelaire, and a number of philosophers.

Modernist theory believes in the breakdown of any linear **narrative structure** which hitherto followed the conventional Aristotelian model of beginning, middle and end. Modern poetry tends to be fragmented, creating its own 'logic' of emotion, image, sound, symbol and mood. Major works of modernist fiction following James Joyce's *Ulysses* and even his more radical

Finnegans Wake (1939) subvert the basic conventions of earlier prose fiction. This was done through breaking up the narrative continuity, departing from the standard ways of representing characters and violating the traditional syntax and coherence of narrative language by using stream of consciousness and other modes of narration. Gertrude Stein, an American writer often linked with Joyce, Pound, Eliot, and Woolf as a trail-blazing modernist, experimented with automatic writing. Such writing achieved its effect by violating the norms of standard English syntax. Peter Barry recapitulates the scenario in these words:

> In all the arts touched by modernism what had been the most fundamental elements of practice were challenged and rejected: thus, melody and harmony were put aside in music; perspective and direct pictorial representation were abandoned in painting, in favour of degree of abstraction; in architecture traditional forms and materials were rejected in favour of plain geometrical forms.... In literature, finally, there was a rejection of traditional realism (chronological plots, continuous narratives relayed by omniscient narrators, 'closed endings', etc.) in favour of experimental forms of various kinds. (82)

The general reader found it difficult to understand modernist writing cause of the fragmentation and lack of conciseness in writing. The plot, characters, and themes of the text are not always linear, making the reader confused about what is being said. A rejection of history, social systems and a sense of loneliness are also **common themes**. Jean Francois Lyotard, the postmodern theoretician, in his report *The Postmodern Condition*, also studies the philosophy of modernism. According to him, modernism was influenced by the Kantian theme of the sublime, which is an equivocal emotion, for it carries with it both pleasure and pain. The sublime is only present when the imagination fails to present an object that could match the concept. "Modern aesthetics is an aesthetic of the sublime, though a nostalgic one. It allows the unpresentable to be put forward only as the missing content; but the form, because of its recognizable consistency, continues to offer to the reader or viewer matter for solace and pleasure." (81). Lyotard feels that we can conceive the infinitely great, the infinitely powerful, but every presentation of an object destined to make visible this absolute greatness or power appears to us painfully inadequate, for these are ideas of which no presentation is possible. Thus, a sense of loss informs modernism. Gary Day concurs with Lyotard and adds:

> We can, then, read modernist art in a number of ways. In part, it is the search for a form of representation adequate to a new kind of society, a search made all the more difficult because the idiom of realism has been commandeered by the institution of mass culture. In part, it is an attempt to keep the value of art separate from that of commerce. And, in part, it is a means of reversing the decline in status of the elite. (265)

However, this desire to secure literature as an **elite preserve** lasted as long as the onset of postmodernism which knocked the bottom out of the elite edifice, by questioning the canon and favouring mass art and popular literature.

Modernism, then, can be summed up as an aesthetic movement of the twentieth century that repudiates the traditional purpose of art to represent reality and address timeless human values. Instead, it holds that the purpose of art is to enable the artist to express his or her emotions, often in an utterly non-representational or abstract manner because the mimetic theory propounded by Aristotle does not work. In literature, it has meant stylistic innovations and dominance over themes which challenged the smugness underlying contemporary human civilization.

Works Cited

Blackbury, Malcolm. *The Social Context of Modern English Literature*. Oxford: Basil Blackwell, 1971.

Day, Gary. *Literary Criticism: A New History*. Edinburgh: Edinhurgh University Press Ltd., 2008, Paperback Edition 2010.

Habib, M.A.R. *Modern Literary Criticism and Theory: A Histotry*. Oxford: Blackwell, 2008.

Lyotard, Jean Francois. "Answering the question: What is Postmodernism?" in *The Postmodern Condition*, Minnesota, U.S.: University of Minnesota Press, 1979, tr. 1984.

Peter Barry. *Beginning Theory: An Introduction to Literary and Cultural Theory*. Manchester, UK: Manchester University Press, 1999.

2

New Criticism

The term 'New Criticism' was first used in 1910 by Joel E. Spingarn in an address at Columbia University. The beginning of this literary critical movement is ascribed to the modernist work of T.S. Eliot, I.A. Richards and F.R. Leavis spread over the second and third decades of the twentieth century. This work found a warm welcome later in the United States among a group of poets, including John Crowe Ransom, Allan Tate, Robert Pen Warren, and Cleanth Brooks. It was here that the foundation of New Criticism was laid with the publication of a book of the same name, i.e. *New Criticism* in 1941 by John Crowe Ransom, an American poet and critic. It remained a prominent feature of the American literary criticism until late 1960s.

The New Critics, as they came to be called, shared the views of their modernist English colleagues about the **contemporary world.** They saw around them a world driven by a desire for material profit. The so-called triumphs of modern science in combination with capitalist greed threatened to destroy traditionand poetry. Writers and critics on both sides of the Atlantic tried to counterbalance the utilitarian and mercenary tendencies. According to the New Critics, due to its formal structure, a poem created harmony out of opposites and tension and thereby presented a vital alternative:

> They grope into the dark of emotional and spiritual bankruptcy only to encounter utter chaos, confusion, and disorder. Bewildered and dejected, standing at a critical juncture, they ultimately turn to take a shelter under the bower of poetry. They cherish a firm faith in poetry as an art and its immense organizing capacity of imagination. With the new critical attitudes of European modernism and literary mannerism and experimentalism, the New Critics, thus, set out to propound the theory of the New Criticism to soothe and structure their fragmented psychic phenomenon. (Munir 49)

It was the chaos and confusion of the early twentieth century which impelled **T.S. Eliot** (1888-1965) to write difficult symbolic poetry to reflect the complexities of his time. *The Waste Land* (1922) is considered a brilliant example of this new type of poetry. His critical corpus consisting of essays showed a new direction to poets and critics. Some of these like "Tradition and the Individual Talent", "The Function of Criticism", "The Frontiers of Criticism", "The Metaphysical Poets" and "Hamlet" not only presented incisive commentary but also advanced the boundary of criticism. Having debunked the focus on individual lives of poets, Eliot focused on the poem itself. This shift in focus was emulated by a number of poets. For this reason, "New Criticism can still be considered amovement, beginning after World War I with the critical work of modern poets and critics, especially T.S. Eliot, Richards and somewhat late Ransom, culminating some 30 years later in the work of explicitly academic critics, such as Wellek, Wimsatt, and Brooks" (Searle 692).

Similarly, **I.A. Richards'** (1893-1979) *Principles of Literary Criticism* (1924) and *Practical Criticism* (1929) were path-breaking books. He showed his aversion to the past critical practices and on the basis of his knowledge of psychology advanced the four-fold theory of sense, feeling, tone and intention in poetry. Through his empirical study, he established in his book *Practical Criticism* that for the critic, the poem is more important than the poet. A poem consists of the words on the page with special effects created through figures of speech and special sounds. This is the principle which gave a fillip to

New Criticism. Thus, the guideposts before the New Critics were the distinction between literature and science as also between content and form. They laid stress on reading a poem as a poem only and treated history, politics and biography of the poet as extraneous.

Cleanth Brooks (1909-94), one of the most scholarly exponents of New Criticism, countered the oft-repeated clichés about poetry, one of which was that poetry is the essence of the best realizations of the best minds. Such a view leads the reader and the critic on a wild goose chase of lofty ideas and messages in poetry. There are suggestions that a poem is a beautiful statement. This, according to Brooks, is not the true function of poetry. Secondly, poetry is often taken to be a substitute for actual experience, as is often suggested by the dictum 'poetry is an experience' which means it is affective or emotional. Brooks debunks these so-called ends of criticism. He believes that none of these—lofty ideas, vivid imagery, rhythm, etc. are poetic in themselves. Poetry can have disagreeable ideas, a halting rhythm and a repulsive imagery; it is the organization of all these parts that matters. Brooks supported his views with insightful essays like "The Language of Paradox" and "Irony as the Principle of Structure".

In creating coherent wholes out of the full variety and contradictory complexity of life, poetry transcends the chaotic flux of actual experience. **John Crowe Ransom** (1888-1974), one of the leading lights of New Criticism, urges that the "emphasis of criticism must move from historical scholarship to aesthetic appreciation and understanding" (Habib 622). He states in his 1937 essay called "Criticism Inc.": "The poet perpetuates in his poem an order of existence which in actual life is constantly crumbling beneath his touch" (597). To accomplish this, one of the poet's main strategies is the use of paradox with irony and wonder. By means of paradoxes, the creative imagination is supposed to achieve union.

In short, the New Critics concentrate on close textual study, on the study of the form, design and texture of poetry. The psychological state of the poet at the time of creation as well as the effect of the poem on readers are not allowed to divert attention from the text. As **William Wimsatt** (1907-75) and **Monroe Beardsley** (1915-85) write in *The Verbal Icon* (1954), "A poem should not/ But be" (from Archibald Macleish's poem 'Ars Poetica'). It means that a poem has an existence as real as the objects around us. But it should captivate the reader like a masterly painting on a wall so that it should not have to explain itself or convey an obvious meaning. A poem conveys a mood, a feeling, a sentiment. The object of critical analysis should be the poem itself. To approach a poem by way of its origins in the mind of its maker or by way of its results in the mind of the audience are fallacies—*intentional fallacy* and *affective fallacy* respectively. The consequence of both these fallacies is that the poem itself, as an object of critical judgment, tends to be ignored.

To the New Critics, therefore, a poem, or a work of art, is the **thing in itself** and is distinct from the poet and his social milieu. The details of the poet's biography and his moral, religious, social, political views are all irrelevant to understand a work of literature. It is a definite entity in itself and must be studied as such. In a poem, form is more important than its content. Words, images, rhythm, metre, etc. constitute the form of poetry and are to be closely studied. These are considered more important than thought, plot or characters in any poem, whether lyrical, narrative or dramatic. Words, besides their literal significance, have emotional and symbolic significance. The elements of metaphor, simile, personification, prosody are important in a poem. Similarly, elements like tone, point of view, narrative structure are important in a narrative poem. Whether it is John Crowe Ransom's principle of 'texture', or Robert Pen Warren's preoccupation with symbols or Allen Tate's theory of 'tension' or Cleanth Brookes 'irony' and 'paradox'—we find the same search for the meaning of words, the way they form the structure of the poem.

That is why a prose paraphrase cannot convey the total meaning of a poem. A poem is an organic whole and the different parts are inter-connected. It is this organic nature of the poem that brings about **harmonization** of conflicting ideas, feelings and attitudes. These interconnections are to be closely followed and examined. The function of the critic is to analyze, interpret, and evaluate a work of art. He must devote himself to close textual study, unhampered by any extraneous concerns. He should look for instances of ambiguity, irony, paradox, etc. The critic must not be prejudiced by any literary theories also. The New Critics are opposed both to the historical and comparative methods of criticism. They are also anti-impressionist. Instead of giving merely his impressions, which are bound to be vague and subjective, the critic must make a close, objective and precise study of the poem concerned.

There is no doubt that New Criticism is **formalistic** and one would think that Russian Formalism influenced it but there are some who negate this possibility: "Considering that the New Critics seem to have known nothing at all about the work of the Formalists and their successors (it is not mentioned at all, for instance, in Wimsatt and Brooks's *Literary Criticism: A Short History* of 1957), these affinities are really very striking.... In contrast to Formalism and Structuralism, the New Criticism was empiricist and humanistic" (Robey 73-74).

The **limitations** of the New Critics were pinpointed by a group of critics who have come to be known as the Chicago Critics, also called Neo-Aristotelians. They are called 'Chicago Critics' because they all worked at the University of Chicago. Ronald Crane is the most important member of the group. Together the group published its views in a volume of essays entitled "Critics and Criticism" (1952). The Chicago School of Critics approach criticism with an open mind and recognize that many different approaches and methods of study can be applied to a work of art. So, it would be wrong to assert that a single approach is correct. The approach of the Chicago Critics is pluralistic (i.e. they use different methods and techniques) as opposed to monistic approach (i.e. use of one method alone) of the New Critics. According to Elder Olson, the critic focusses on one or the other facet of the poem or he studies several facets at the same time. But the New Critics are too much occupied with textual analysis. Moreover, the New Critical approach has been mainly tried in the field of poetry. These critics have not ventured much into the field of fiction or drama.

We can conclude with the observation that a work of art is generally believed to also have other functions like the aesthetic and the moralappeal. Then, textual analysis, as T.S. Eliot, pointed out, can establish only the literary quality of a work, and to determine its greatness other methods are also necessary. Overmuch stress on textual element in poetry can lead to 'lemon-squeezer criticism', as Eliot put it. Moreover, it is not necessary that the social, biographical and historical factors will not contribute to our understanding of the meaning; these may also help in determining the meaning of a literary text.

Works Cited

John Crowe Ransom. "Criticism Inc.", *The Virginia Quarterly Review*, Autumn 1937, pp. 587-602. 17 June 2013 <http://www.vqronline.org/articles/1937/autumn/ransom-criticism-inc/>.

Munir. *The New Criticism*. New Delhi: Adhyayan, 2011.

Robey, David. "The Anglo-American New Criticism", *Modern Literary Theory: A Comparative Introduction*, Eds. London: Batsford, 1986, pp. 73-91.

Searle, Leroy, F. "New Criticism", *The John Hopkins Guide to Literary Theory & Criticism*, Second Edition. Eds. Groden, Michael et al. Baltimore: The John Hopkins University Press, 2005.

3

Russian Formalism

During the second decade of the twentieth century, the Russian Formalists inspired by their predecessors, and under the banner of the Formalist Linguistic Circle of Moscow, took up cudgels against undue focus on the author in literary criticism. They favoured an approach based upon analysis of the language of a text in relation to its psychological effect on the reader. To say that literature was nothing but form and that it was form that provided meaning to content was indeed a revolutionary idea and it is opined by many that the pioneers of this thinking were inspired by the Russian Revolution and wanted to revolutionize literature also. Among the scholars associated with this school were Victor Shklovsky, Boris Eichenbaum and Roman Jakobson. The Moscow group comprised of linguists, literary critics and psychologists who later developed the foregrounding theory.

"The earliest beginnings of Russian Formalism can be dated from 1914", says Ann Jefferson, "with the appearance of Viktor Shklovsky's essay on Futurist poetry, 'The Resurrection of the Word'" (24). There were **two schools** of Russian Formalism:the Moscow Linguistic Circle, led by Roman Jakobson formed in 1915 and the Society for the Study of Poetic Language founded in 1916. While Roman Jakobson belonged to the first school, Victor Shklovsky and Boris Eichenbaum were the prominent figures belonging to the second. Other important Formalist critics are Yuri Tynianov, Boris Tomashevsky, Vladimir Propp, Mikhail Bakhtin and Jan Mukarovsky.

The Russian Formalists' work could not reach the Western academies simultaneously because of the 1917 Bolshevik Revolution that transformed the Czar-ruled Russia into the Communist-party ruled Soviet Union. The Communist regime which came to power was hostile to the Formalist movement because of latter's indifference to social context. Despite the fact that during the 1920s, the Formalist critics moved from pure formalism to greater concern with societal context, this movement could not resist pressure from the Stalinist regime and came to an end around the 1930s but by that time it had added an important chapter in the domain of literary criticism.

In the meantime, critics I.A. Richards, William Empson, Ezra Pound and T.S. Eliot inspired a new movement in the U.S.A. which came to be known as **New Criticism.** Both the Russian Formalists and the New Critics decried the prevailing tendency to delve deep into the biographies of writers while assessing their work. But the New Critics had their influence after the Russian Formalists had disappeared from the scene due mainly to domestic political pressure. The effective period of influence of the New Critics is reckoned to be from 1930s to 1960s. However, it was the seeds of Russian Formalism brought over to the U.S.A. by critics like Roman Jakobson and Rene Wallek which helped New Criticism to grow. For this reason, the New Critics are also sometimes referred to as American Formalists. The New Critics also focussed on features like irony, paradox and metaphor, but they did not apply the science of linguistics to poetry as the Russian Formalists did. So, whereas the New Critics became interested in the way a technique revealed the thematic aspect of a work, the Russian Formalists studied the technique used in literature for its own sake. The Formalists' analyses were far more theoretical. They sought to understand the general nature of literary devices as well as the historical evolution of literary techniques. On the other hand, the New Critics were more concerned with the practice (rather than theory) of close reading of individual texts.

The growth of Russian Formalism can be divided in **two phases.** At the initial stage, the Russian Formalists presented a simplified definition of the literary work as a sum of its poetic devices, but later, they viewed individual text as a more elaborate system in which the internal elements affected each other in complex ways and which had to be viewed in the context created by other works. Raman Seldon remarks in this context: "The first Russian Formalists on the other hand considered that human 'content' (emotions, ideas, and 'reality' in general) possessed no literary significance in itself, but merely provided a context for the functioning of literary 'devices'" (6). The formalists had a scientific approach to literature like the structuralists. Both believed that poetry is a special function of language only. They aimed at studying the 'literariness' behind literature. One could discover the underlying formulae or structures of literary texts by studying 'devices' like rhythm, alliteration, imagery and symbolism. To them, poetic language is different in that it does not perform the usual referential function as is does in other disciplines like natural sciences or social sciences, but 'foregrounds' itself in literature, i.e. language becomes an end in itself and is self-reflexive. Therefore, "To read a poem is to read an arrangement of sounds and words that looks different and that means differently from ordinary speech or the ordinary use of the same words. Literature changes ordinary language by roughening it up so that the words draw attention to themselves" (Ryan 3).

The formalists opposed the Aristotelian mimetic theory and, in its place, favoured **'defamiliarization'** in literature. Literature is no longer seen as aiming to represent reality or character or to impart moral or intellectual lessons. Rather, it is considered to be an object in its own right, possessing its own laws and objectives internal to itself. Moreover, from the formalist view, literature does not convey any clear or paraphrasable message. Literature is regarded as a unique mode of expression. The formalist approach has nothing to do with history and biography. It isolates the literary artifact from both broad social forces and personal circumstances of its author. Moreover, the

Russian Formalists also argued that if a new form evolved, then it also changed the content of the genre. To quote Michael Ryan,

> The form of the medieval quest romance—long poems with chivalric characters and religious themes—determines the range of characters and ideas one would be likely to encounter in such works. Cervantes' use of a picaresque narrative style in *Don Quixote*, a new post-romance kind of novel which strings adventures together with seeming randomness, is a formal development that accounts for or motivates the pliability of his hero, Don Quixote. (3)

They aimed at explaining how aesthetic effects are produced by literary devices. Literary devices were 'deviations' from everyday speech. The early formalist critics tended to identify 'literariness' with poetical effects and therefore, studied the rhythmic patterns, syntax, structure, imagery, etc. that distinguish a literary work from other written or spoken discourses. For the formalists, the proper province of criticism is the 'literariness' of a text and not the content. The sharp division of form and content was modified by the later formalists. It is a fact that most of the formalists were in their twenties or thirties when they expressed their views and as it was with Wordsworth, who gushed over French Revolution during his youth but mellowed down in middle age, the formalists too toned down their extreme positions later. Some of the formalists, particularly Viktor Shklovsky, Vladimiar Propp and Tzvetan Todorov took up the study of fiction, in which they analyzed narratives and identified strategies which had been used for long in plot construction even in the myths. It was a new insight into literature that went a long way and developed the area of narratology. Mikhail Bakhtin marked the distinction between poetry and fiction by arguing that the former was a single voice but the latter was a complex of voices, which he called 'heteroglossia'.

Thus, the formalists have made impressive contribution to the **theory of fiction.** With respect to this genre, the central formalist distinction is between 'story' (the simple enumeration of chronological sequence of events) and 'plot'. An author is said to transform the raw material of a story into a literary plot through the use of a variety of devices that violate sequence and defamiliarize the elements of a story. The effect is to foreground the narrative medium and devices. Since each one of the formalists had his individual viewpoint also besides his allegiance to broad contours of formalism, it would be fruitful to review their contribution in detail here.

Roman Jakobson (1896-1982), a brilliant student of Moscow University, was a member of the Moscow Linguistic Circle. His work occupies a central and seminal place in the development of formalism. In 1926, Jakobson founded the Prague Linguistic Circle which critically engaged with the work of Saussure. He argues that poetics is an integral part of linguistics: "The object of study in literary science is not literature but literariness, that is, what makes a given work a literary work" (Abrams 114). He contributed to the study of phonology and was one of the earliest linguists to analyse the sound system. His work also underlined the importance of metaphor and metonymy. Jakobson's essay "Two Aspects of Language and Two Types of Aphasic Disturbances" (1956) draws attention to the fact that language has a bipolar structure. Its two poles are the metaphor and the metonymy. The development of any discourse takes place along two semantic lines: one is metaphoric, where one topic leads to another through similarity or substitution and the other is metonymic where one topic suggests another via contiguity (closeness in space, time, or psychological association). He also explains that metaphor inspires romanticism while metonymy supports realistic literature.

An equally important figure is **Victor Shklovsky** (1893-1984). He rejected the notion that literature is based on imagery alone. In his essay "Art as Technique" (1917), he propounded the notion of 'defamiliarization' which was taken as one of the central statements of the formalist theory. He argued that we can never retain the freshness of our perceptions of objects. As our normal perceptions become habitual, they become automatic and unconscious. Things are replaced by symbols. We fail to apprehend the object, which fades and does not leave even the first impression of the object. Art, for Shklovsky, is a way of experiencing the artfulness of an object even where the object is not important. As an illustration of 'defamiliarization', he quoted Tolstoy's story *Kholstomer*, in which a horse describes the world of humans. Also Shklovsky hails Leo Tolstoy's *War and Peace* for defamiliarizing of opera by a person in the audience who is unaware of the conventions of anopera. Thus, the point of view as a literary device brings about literary difference vis-à-vis non-literary writing. Shklovsky greatly admired Laurence Sterne's novel *Life and Opinions of Tristram Shandy, Gentleman* for its comic undercurrent and flouting of novelistic conventions. In his acclaimed essay "Sterne's *Tristram Shandy*: Stylistic Commentary", he showed that Sterne reflects self-awareness of literary form when he jumps into the narrative to inform the reader that the story had been following a particular course and that thereafter it would take a different course. Clearly, the stress here is on stylistic and formalistic elements rather than on the content.

Long before the Western linguists arrived on the scene, the Russian scholar **Vladimir Propp** (1895-1970) undertook a study of numerous folklores and their categorization in his *Morphology of the Folk Tale* (1928, translated 1958), which became an epoch-making treatise. He zeroed in on seven 'spheres of action' and thirty-one fixed 'functions' of narrative. His heroes, creating these spheres of action, are: hero, false hero, villain, donor/provider, helper, princess and her father, and dispatcher.

Propp's compatriot **Mikhail Bakhtin** (1895-1975) contributed a lot to Narratology. He believed language to be basically dialogic because language made sense only in communication. Writing under the name of his friend V.N. Voloshinov, he focussed on parole rather than langue. His essay "Discourse in the Novel" (1934) deals with both his philosophy of language and theory of language. In this essay, Bakhtin defines novel as a diversity of social speech types (sometimes identified with the diversity of languages) and diversity of individual voices, artistically organized. The word 'dialogue' in its everyday usage means verbal interchange between individuals. It is the central feature of all speech and so a novel foregrounds the dialogic aspect of speech and everyday communication. Meaning of any utterance depends on the social context. Novel is also the example of *heteroglossia*, which means different levels of language and dialogue. All voices in a polyphonic work like a novel are given equal importance. The novel is also the site of struggle and subversion. He described it through the metaphor of *carnival*. This notion was evolved by him on the basis of his study of French Renaissance writer Rabelais's works. Carnival, per se, refers to some extravagant festivity in which both commoners and privileged classes are temporarily free to transgress all kinds of social and religious norms. The carnival stands for laughter, bodily functions (urination, defecation), parody, grotesqueness and lowliness. This feature is always inscribed in the mass culture and in it people are both spectators and participants. Subversion of authority is indicated by carnival which is also described as the 'ultimate other' and it defies theorization. Bakhtin also presents the concept of intertextuality in its nascent form.

Boris Eichenbaum (1886-1959) was another leader of the Russian Formalist group known as The Society for the Study of Poetic Language founded in 1916. He presented his views on both poetry and fiction. In his *Melody of Russian Lyric Verse* (1923), he studied the poetic intonation as it evolved through the interaction between rhythm and syntax. In his famous essay on Gogol's "Overcoat", he analyzed the story without reference to extra literary referents. He expressed the view that it was the 'telling' of the story or *skaz*, as he called it, which produced a grotesque effect on the reader by dishing out irrelevant detail and shifting the tone suddenly from comic to pathetic. In his seminal essay, "The Theory of the 'Formal Method'" (1926-27), he expounded the evolution of the central principles of the formalist methodology. He stated that formalism is "characterized only by an attempt to create an independent science of literature which studies specifically literary materials". He also argued that poetry uses words differently from their function in ordinary speech. The formalists also rejected the idea of some linear, unified tradition in literary history, rather they believed that literary tradition involved struggle, destruction of old values and competition between various schools in a given epoch and therefore could not be relied upon as a model.

Yuri Tynianov (1894-1943) co-authored with Jakobson *The Theses on Language* in 1928. He believed that the distinction between synchrony and diachrony was useful for the study of literature as for language, but each synchronic system also had its own past and future as part of its structure. In an essay "Dostoevsky and Gogol: Toward a Theory of Parody" published in 1921, he shows how, while following Nikolai Gogol, Fyodor M. Dostoevsky (1821-81) produced a parody and thereby initiated a new form of his own. Similarly, in his essay "On Literary Evolution" published in 1927, he outlined his views on literary change, which, according to him, involved evolution of the total literary system. With the change in the thinking of a literary school, the defining characteristics of a genre or mode also underwent change, so much so that even the forms once considered non-literary are accepted in literature in due course of time. Clearly, he presaged postmodern literature here.

One of the foundational essays of Russian Formalism was "Thematics", which was penned by Boris **Tomashevsky** (1866-1939). He distinguishes between two kinds of arrangements: thematic elements that are ordered by causal temporal relationships from stories (narratives, tales, novels); and those that are contemporaneous. Working on narratology, he distinguished between *fabula* (story) and *suzhet* (pronounced as 'soojay', meaning plot) which were introduced by Shklovsky in 1921 (Bertens 36). Whereas fabula is the actual sequence of events as they happened, *syuzhet* is the re-arrangement of details carried out to create the literary effect. He was also fascinated by the literary device of defamiliarization which he found most pronounced in Jonathan Swift's *Gulliver's Travels*. When Gulliver visits the land ruled by horses, he tells them about human society and the socio-political order in it. His method of telling is such that by removing the usual euphemistic terminology, the whole thing appears defamiliarized and horrible. In his "Russian Versification: Metrics" published in 1923, Tomashevsky laid down the principles for a statistical study of verse features which achieved canonical status in Russian literary criticism.

In conclusion, it can be said that Russian Formalism represents one of the earliest attempts to put literary studies on a scientific footing. Russian Formalism influenced American theories of stylistics and narratology. American New Criticism, also referred to as American Formalism sometimes, shares many characteristics with Russian Formalism but the former tends to bestow aesthetic form with moral and cultural significance. Russian Formalism set the pace for structuralism also, as is evident from the following observation: "The main influence of Russian and Czech formalism on American criticism has been on the development of stylistics and of narratology. Roman Jakobson and Tzvetan Todorov have also been influential in introducing Formalist concepts and methods into French structuralism" (Abrams, 116).

Works Cited

Abrams, M.H. and Geoffrey Galt Harpham. *A Handbook of Literary Terms*. New Delhi: Cengage Learning, 2009.

Bertnes, Hans. *Literary Theory: The Basics*. London: Routledge, 2001.

Jefferson, Ann and David Robey, eds. *Modern Literary Theory: A Comparative Introduction*. London: Batsford, 1986.

Ryan, Michael. *Literary Theory: A Practical Introduction*. New York: Blackwell, 1999, Indian Reprint 2002.

Selden, Raman. *A Reader's Guide to Contemporary Literary Theory*. Sussex: Harvester, 1985.

4

Structuralist Criticism

Inspired by Ferdinand de Saussure's *Course in General Linguistics* (1916), structuralism first appeared as an approach in linguistics and a decade later, it turned into a literary and social theory impacting anthropology, political theory, philosophy, religion, history, economics, psychology, etc. Not only this, as a world view, structuralism connotes a system of structures and sub-structures in the world. A structuralist's job is to look for a set of variables capable of generating all possible structures. It is an analytical method. Various systems—literature, kinship, clothing or traffic signals—all operate according to codes or sets of rules just like the rules that are applied to language. According to Robert Kellogg, structuralism seeks the unification of all sciences into a new system of belief so that the codes governing other systems can be studied with the same scientific precision and by using many of the concepts of language (287). Structuralism appeared at a time when existentialism and Marxism dominated the scene and quite a few votaries of existentialism became followers of structuralism. In literature, its impact was felt most between 1940 and 1960, but even now, it continues to have influence on linguistics and narratology.

Structuralist Criticism is so-called because the critics subscribing to this school analyze literature on the model of structuralist **linguistics**. This class of critics includes a number of Russian Formalists, especially Roman Jakobson, and some prominent French critics. It was in the later 1920s that Jakobson and some other Russian Formalists left Russia at the height of the civil war between the supporters and antagonists of the Bolshevik Party, and moved to Prague (Czechoslovakia) where they founded the Prague Linguistic Circle in 1926. In fact, the Russian Formalists provided the lead, but due to turmoil in Russian politics and its virtual alienation from the world, these were some European and American schools which advanced the study of literary structuralism. Thus, the Linguistic Circles of Prague and Copenhagen, French Formalism, American Bloomfieldians and New Criticism, British Functionalism and Practical Criticism, etc. have all contributed to the evolution of structuralism.

Further, it must be added here that the structuralists replaced defamiliarization of the Russian Formalists by the **foregrounding** theory. Poetic language was believed to be an effect of the foregrounding of the utterance, i.e. it drew the reader's attention to itself. Some of the well-known practitioners of this school of thought included, besides Roman Jakobson, his disciple Claude Levi Strauss (whom he taught in New York when the former migrated to the U.S.A. in 1941), Jan Mukarovsky, Roland Barthes, Jacques Lacan, Todorov, etc.

The foremost reason for the development of structuralism was the rising scientific tendency of the age. The conventional view of literature including the value of language, the aesthetics of literature, the role of the author, literary history and biography were all subjected to review. Modern literary theories attacked the underlying assumptions of the Anglo-American critical tradition. A kind of coherence and order was sought to be brought to literary studies which appeared to the structuralists as formless and chaotic.

The following are, in a nutshell, the **key features** and beliefs of structuralism:

1. It is opposed to mimetic and expressive theories of literature.
2. It is not an interpretive theory, it looks for grammar of literature and its poetics. It posits literature to literariness as language to linguistics.

3. Units or individual things can be understood in the context of larger structures only. Thus, literature is considered as part of culture.
4. The relationships are most often described in terms of binary oppositions.
5. The author, as traditionally understood, is dead. The subject is constructed by linguistic system.
6. An author's work is re-defined as an impersonal text.
7. It is neither the writer nor the writing but language that speaks now.
8. Focus is on reading and production of meaning based upon linguistic conventions (words, phrases, sentences, etc.).

Structuralism is **different from formalism,** which is concerned with the form and structure and not the meaning or content of a literary work. In the structuralist approach, although formal elements in literary works constitute an important part, yet structuralism is not confined to this aspect alone. It seeks to explore the relationship between the system of literature and the human culture of which it is a part. An important point of difference with Russian Formalism is that structuralism banks heavily on linguistics as propounded by Ferdinand de Saussure, who is widely acclaimed as the 'father' of modern linguistics as his ideas have proved to be seminal to the semiological orientation of linguistics. He was the first to introduce the concept of structure in language. In his *Course in General Linguistics*, he offered an in-depth study of the nature of language and linguistic structure. Linguists believe that the meaning of a word lies in linguistic system and not in the word, since the word is a signifier and it has no inherent or natural linkage with the signified. For arriving at the meaning of a word, one has to take into account the linguistics evolved in a particular community. Unless one knows about the language system which governs the meaning of an utterance, one cannot comprehend it.

Saussure made it clear that the nature of the subject here was semiological, i.e. based upon signs and the relationship between the signifier (the sound-image—spoken sound or mental image created while reading) and the signified (the concept or thing) is essentially arbitrary. He emphasized the importance of considering language as a system. The term given by him for the purpose is 'langue' as opposed to the individual speech act or 'parole'. Another term 'langage' was explained by him as the entire human potential for speech. Further, he dwelt on the need to define linguistic entities relationally, i.e. in terms of the ways in which they combine with or are opposed to each other. In short, he elaborated the distinctions between: (i) signifier and signified, (ii) langue and parole, (iii) synchronic and diachronic analyses, and (iv) paradigmatic and syntagmatic relationships. The structuralist notion propounded by Saussure shifted the focus from the relation between texts and world or between texts and meaning to the study of literary process aimed at deciphering the production of meaning in a text. M.A.R. Habib underlines the importance of Saussure's views thus: "This view of language also challenges the view of reality as somehow independent and existing outside of language, reducing language to merely a 'name-giving system.' Saussure's view implies that we build up an understanding of our world by means of language and view the world through language" (71).

Roman Jakobson (1896-1982) formulated what is probably the ultimate attempt to define the aesthetic function of poetry, that is, the **'literariness'** (that what makes a given work a work of literature) of poetry. "The poetic function", Jakobson said, "projects the principle of equivalence from the axis of selection into the axis of combination" (38). The selection process starts with our selecting words from large classes of grammatically equivalent words: nouns, verbs, adjectives, and so on. We make a selection from a number of words that have much in common and even if they are roughly identical, they are approximately or wholly equivalent in meaning. Alliteration, for example, is an equivalence between sounds, as for example, in Emily Dickinson's poem "The Soul Selects Her Own Society" (Johnson 143), we find the sound /s/ repeated in words. Poetry can also create equivalence by means of rhyme. But it can also do so by way of meter. Jakobson wedded language to literature by relating syntagmatic and paradigmatic axes to the use of metaphor and metonymy in literature. He explained that metaphor inspires romanticism and metonymy is prominent in realistic literature. While the romantic poet searches for an unrelated image that might stand in place of the original, the realist author digresses from plot to the related atmosphere and from characters to setting in space and time. Thus, in painting, cubism is metonymic and surrealism is metaphorical. In literature, poetry is metaphorical because it fiddles with paradigmatic possibilities and prose is metonymic as it is more concerned with syntagmatic progression.

It is a truism that all battles targetting literature have been fought in the name of search for reality. Structuralism is no exception. The structuralists believed that literature did not reflect reality or life because the language consisting of signs does not refer to objects; rather it refers to other signs only. The earlier view that language yields its contents or meaning without any modification was now under attack. The structuralists were interested in comprehending the conventions which were responsible for our arriving at the meaning. They also looked for general principles lying at the roots of individual attempts in literature. Naturally, form became more important than meaning. Literature was wrenched out of its socio-cultural context. The structuralists sought to provide a scientific basis to literature. They considered literature akin to language insofar as the structures were concerned.

The structuralists discovered the surface and deep **levels in literature** as in language. At the surface or manifest level are the genres like novels and poems, and at the deeper, latent systemic level, we have characters, images, words and the rules of form or the grammar of language to apply. The structure of literature, they felt, can be compared to that of langue and parole. Structuralist critics have focused on prose narratives which they take as an extension of the sentence structure. They have been able to point out some universal narrative structures. Roman Jakobson calls the conventions behind the production of literature, as the langue of literature and Todorov calls it the grammar of literature. Noam Chomsky calls them 'universal underlying structures'.

Structuralist narratology has made good progress. In this connection, Russian Formalist Vladimir Propp's (1896-1970) *The Morphology of the Fòlktale* identifies some 35 'functions' and seven 'spheres of action' in Russian folk stories. Propp's character typology reduces the indefinite number of characters to a finite number of basic structural agents including villain, donor, helper, princess, hero, and false hero. In this context, Michael Ryan's observation is pertinent: "Much as verbs always follow subjects and sometimes take objects, actions in fiction obey similar rules of consistency" (26).

Similar to Propp's character typology, **Myth Criticism** exposes patterns of myth, as for example, the mother-son relationship and patricide in the myth of Oedipus as deep structures underlying a variety of texts. The most famous and influential example of this approach is J.G. Frazer's (1954-41) work *The Golden Bough*, which tries to reveal the common structures of myths in different historical periods and geographical areas. Claude Levi-Strauss (1908-2009) in his book *Structural Anthropology* (1958) also refers to basic mythological patterns in its description and analysis of cultures. The most influential contribution offered by mythological approach to literary criticism is the work of Northrop Frye (1912-91). He places structures of myth at the heart of what he considers the main literary genres. According to Frye, the forms of comedy, romance, tragedy and irony (i.e. satire) resemble the patterns of seasons (spring, summer, autumn and winter, respectively) in primordial myths.

Archetypal Criticism, based on C.G. Jung's (1875-1961) theory, works along similar lines by searching texts for collective motifs of the human psyche. They are held to be common to different historical periods and languages. These archetypes represent primordial images of the human unconscious which have retained their structures in various cultures and epochs. Archeytpes such as shadow, fire, snake, paradise-garden, hell, mother-figure, etc. constantly surface in myth and literature as a limited number of basic patterns of psychic images which lend themselves to a structural mode of explanation.

Roland Barthes (1915-80) also extended structural analysis and semiology (the study of signs) to the broad cultural phenomena. In his book *Mythologies* (1957), Barthes undertook an ideological critique of various products of bourgeois culture—ranging from soap to advertising. Barthes' most fundamental suggestion is that myth is not an object, a concept, or an idea but a language, a type of speech. It is a mode of signification. In explaining the nature of myth, Barthes reiterates Saussure's view that semiology is comprised of three (rather than two) terms: the *signifier*, which is an acoustic (sound) image, the *signified*, which is a concept, and the *sign*, which is a word and which consists of the combination of signifier and signified. Barthes's study of Balzac's story "Sarrasine" in his 'S/Z' is an example of the structural method of literary analysis. Barthes divides the story into 561 units of meaning called lexia. These units are classified using five codes. Similarly, Griemas' 'universal grammar of narrative' proposes three binary oppositions: subject/object; sender/receiver; helper/opponent, etc.

A structuralist criticism of *King Lear* would look upon the theme as a conflict between good and evil. The characters would also symbolize different qualities and perform the function to advance the plot *a la* Propp's narratology. Thus, the characters and the dialectical theme perform functions to advance the plot of the story. The observation by Jonathan Culler would be apt here:

> The type of literary work which structuralism helps one to envisage would not be primarily interpretive; it would not offer a method which when applied to literary works, produced new and hitherto unexpected meanings, it would be a poetics which strives to define the conditions of meaning. Granting new attention to the activity of reading, it would attempt to specify how we go about making sense of texts, what are the interpretive operations on which literature itself, as an institution, is based. (Culler xiv)

Structuralist narratology based on structuralist principles has come a long way. The traditional belief is that the work of literature is the product of an author's creative life and expresses the author's essential self. The text is the place where we enter into a spiritual or humanistic communion with an author's thoughts and feelings. Structuralist approaches challenge such cherished beliefs of the ordinary reader. Structuralists have tried to persuade the reader that the author is 'dead'. The overtly scientific attitude of the structuralists to the study of literature and their attempt to create a 'science' of literary studies has not gone well with litterateurs and critics. Barthes was probably the first structuralist to show signs of skepticism when he analysed Balzac's story "Sarrasine". The approach was called post-structuralist. He hardly dwelt on the fixed structuralist framework of the story; he rather showed infinite ways of analyzing the story. Many French thinkers of the 50s and 60s were being seen as post-structuralists during the 70s. Structuralism survives now mainly in stylistics and narratology.

Works Cited

Culler, Jonathan. *Structuralist Poetics*. London: Routledge, 1975, Indian Reprint 2012.

Habib, M.A.R. *A History of Literary Criticism*. Oxford: Blackwell Publishing, 2005, Indian Reprint, 2006.

Jakobson, Roman. "Linguistics and Poetics", *Modern Criticism and Theory: A Reader*. Harlow, Ed. David Lodge. UK: Longman, 2000.

Johnson, Thomas H. ed. *The Complete Poems of Emily Dickinson*. Delhi: Kalyan, 1960.

Kellogg, Robert et al. *The Nature of Narrative*. New York: Oxford, 2006.

Ryan, Michael. *Literary Theory: A Practical Introduction*. New York: Blackwell, 1999, Indian Reprint 2002.

5

Poststructuralism and Deconstruction

Postmodernism, as a wide encompassing term, refers to human culture—to a way of thinking, life style and all human constructs like language and literature, poststructuralism is related to language, literature and other academic areas like social sciences. These might be viewed as two perspectives: Whereas the perspective of postmodernism situates modern theory within the context of larger economic and cultural tendencies, poststructuralism on the other hand, can be seen as a reaction against as well as extension of the structuralist modes of analysis, including literature and political theory. Both postmodernism and poststructuralism believe in ontological uncertainty and relativity. Both question grand theories and grand narratives and for that matter, this thinking informs all disciplines so that politics, history, sociology, psychology and even science are all considered fiction.

Poststructuralism started as a **reaction to structuralism** when it rejected the centrality of structure as propounded by Saussure. Cuddon is right in saying that it is a "more rigorous working out of the possibilities, implications and shortcomings of structuralism and its basis in Saussurian linguistics itself" (690). In the Saussurian linguistic model of the sign, the signified is arbitrarily linked to the signifier and does not directly refer to the object. Moreover, the sign gets its meaning from its relation to other signs. It leads to the conclusion that meaning is relational and not inherent; it is a function of language rather than a reflection of reality. Consequently, it is possible to change reality by describing it differently. Since it is not rooted in reality, it is indeterminate. Taking cue from it, poststructuralism places highest value on language. It believes that truth and reality are linguistic in nature, for "there is nothing outside the text". All our areas of knowledge like religion, politics and literature are also constructs of language. There is no thought possible at the pre-language level. Like the unstable sign—the basic feature of language—all constructs of language are also unstable.

The arrival of poststructuralism was announced by the Algeria-born French scholar **Jacques Derrida** (1930-2004), when he presented his paper "Structure, Sign and Play in the Discourse of Human Sciences" in 1966 at John Hopkins University, in the form of a kind of semiotic analysis called Deconstruction. Derrida attacked Saussure's concept of the structure of language, as represented by the anthropologist Claude Levi-Strauss. Derrida asserted that the notion of a systematic structure presupposes a fixed 'centre' that serves to organize and regulate the structure, yet itself remains outside the structure. This is because the centre is imagined as a 'transcendental signified' which occupies the supreme status as the giver of meaning and cannot itself be questioned. This obsession has been termed logocentrism by Derrida after the word logos, one of whose meanings is the 'word of God'. In the Derridean scheme of things, logos could be anything—God, truth, essence, idea, centre, a principle, etc.

Just as Derrida denies the special status of the logos and its exclusion with regard to the elements of structure, he also takes up the structural elements found to be in the form of binaries like light/dark, presence/absence, man/woman, etc. in which the term on the left is prioritized over the term on the right. Since the sign is unstable and relational, there is no point in taking the two parts of a binary as representing extreme positions. A binary forms a violent hierarchy and the bias in it can be judged from the observation that "the valued terms are truth (defined as the presence of ideas or of objects in the mind), reason, rationality, meaning, logic, authenticity, originality, speech, immediacy, the living, identity, etc. The devalued terms are difference, signification, non-identity, repetition, substitution, writing, imitation, representation, artifice, metaphor, etc." (Ryan 72).

Now, this kind of preference for a term from the first set over the corresponding term in the second set is not an innocent act. Actually, the first term in any binary, say for example, in light/dark requires the other as well to explain itself. This means 'light' itself cannot be self-identical; it has to depend upon 'dark' to have an identity for itself. There is, therefore, no logic in prioritizing one over the other. Thus, speech has always been wrongly prioritized over writing because to us, speech assures the presence of the speaker, whereas writing comes later and is, therefore, taken to be a second order of signification. Derrida calls it phonocentrism, which is a form of logocentrism here.

Derrida enunciated the tool of deconstruction, which was also used by other poststructuralists. The vital difference between Saussurean structuralism and poststructuralism lies in this that whereas Saussure believed that having once arbitrarily linked **signified to signifier**, the relationship became permanent for a sign and became its meaning, Derrida challenged this notion and established that the signifier (name) did not lead to signified (object/concept) because all that it does is to refer to other signifiers in the language, and the other signifier leads to yet another signifier, and the process continues endlessly, for there is nothing outside the language. For example, a simple search in the dictionary for the meaning of the world 'meaning' will make it clear. This is the probable trajectory of search: the meaning given is 'what is meant', but when one looks for the meaning of 'meant', one comes across 'past participle of mean'. Thus, we reach from where we began in a Catch-22 situation!

Derrida names this process **'differance'**—a coinage from the French word *differer*, which means both 'to differ'—in space and 'to defer'—in time. The journey ad infinitum of signifiers does not lead to any fixed meaning because what one gets in this transference is a 'different' signifier, which 'defers' the search for the signified. There is always an element of undecidability or what he calls 'play' here. But how do we arrive at the meaning then? His answer is that the apparent meaning—for the meaning is never final—lies in the 'trace' left behind by evanescent sign, which he describes in his inimitably metaphorical language: "The trace simultaneously traced and erased; simultaneously living and dead and as always living in its simulation of life's preserved inscription. A pyramid, not a stone fence jumped over but itself stone-like on wall, to be deciphered, otherwise a text without voice" (Derrida: 1982, 24). Now, this nature of 'trace' is quite ambivalent, has a play and it might even lead to aporia, or a dead-end in logic. Elsewhere, Derrida describes it thus: "The Chain of signification becomes the trace of presence-absence" (Derrida: 1976, 71). Thus, with the postulates of *differeance and trace*—features of sign or language—Derrida questions the absoluteness of truth on the basis of language.

> ...there is no 'truth' or 'reality' which somehow stands outside or behind languge; truth is a relation of linguistic terms, and reality is a construct, ultimately religious, social, political, and economic, but always of language, of various linguistic registers. Even the human self, in this view, has no pregiven essence but is a linguistic construct or narrative. (Habib 652)

As for the **methodology** employed to deconstruct a text, it focusses on a close reading of the text's language to find its logos or presuppositions, its irrational binaries and point to the aporias:

> The deconstructive reading directs our attention in the text to where some cardinal concepts are seen to rest on slippery grounds. This reading will further reveal how some seemingly marginal details of the text upset the entire logic of its construction. One result of such reading is undoubtedly to challenge the commonplace assumption that philosophy has to do with concepts, truth-claims, logical arguments, in short, with clear and distinct ideas. (Batra 16)

If Derrida was inclined towards the working of language as the foundation of all knowledge, **Michel Foucault** (1926-84), another French philosopher and critic, deconstructed the power of the word and laid bare the political nature of discourse. He started out as a researcher in the field of mental ailment and prison reforms. In his early books *Madness and Civilization* (1961) and *The Birth of the Clinic* (1963), he noted that the general viewpoint regarding the treatment meted out to mentally insane persons was considered to be an enlightened approach over the harsh ways of the preceding ages, but he found in madness a challenge to conventional social norms. He criticized the so-called scientific systems of clinical medicine and imprisonment. He located at the back of these measures the power of discourse which labelled some people mad and others sane.

In the field of literary criticism, Foucault re-defined the concept of **discourse** which brings in the context of the text. He argued that the analysis of a literary text could not be limited to the text or to the author's background only. Instead, it should cover a larger context including the cultural practices in which a text is produced. To quote a critic, "Poststructuralism seems to present at least two distinct family resemblances. The deconstructive textualism centred at Yale, and the political contexualism to be found in various manifestations almost everywhere else" (Felperin 158). Traditionally, the term 'discourse' was used for passages representing conversations between characters in a literary work. In poststructural criticism, discourse has become an important term among critics who oppose the deconstructive concept of a 'general text' that functions independently of particular historical conditions. Instead, they consider discourse to be social parlance, or 'language-in-use' in society.

Foucault qualifies discourse as conditioned by the power structure in society. In his essay 'The Order of Discourse' (1970), he remarks, "In every society the production of discourse is at once controlled, selected, organized and redistributed by a certain number of procedures whose role is to ward off its powers and dangers, to gain mastery over its chance events, to evade its ponderous, formidable materiality" (52). Further, Foucault explains that even though discourse is the context of all speech, knowledge and representation, it remains **anonymous in circulation** in society, "situated at the level of the 'it is said' (on dit)" (qtd. in Abrams 242). Foucault had a great impact on the poststructural approaches like New Historicism, Queer Theory and the broader area of Cultural Studies. It can be understood as an example that when the New Historicists make use of anonymous material as basis for judgement, they are actually depending upon discourse. So, the existing power structure in a society creates a discourse which shapes the thinking of most people who accept it as a 'given' or as something to be accepted without questioning.

It may be pointed out here that Derrida does not agree with Foucault on this point and describes discourse as language without a logos/centre, where everything becomes a system of differences only. Thus, while Derrida based his 'reading strategy', as he calls it, of deconstruction upon linguistic (read semiological) consideration, Foucault linked it to the unseen network of ideas guiding general thinking on a subject.

In his seminal essay "What is an Author?" (1966), Foucault opposed the valorization of author. Whereas writing has been considered as a means of immortalizing the author, Foucault thought differently and placed discourse above author as well as text. Regarding writing, he had startling views:

> Writing is now linked to sacrifice and to the sacrifice of life itself; it is a voluntary obliteration of the self that does not require representation in books because it takes place in the everyday existence of the writer. Where a work had the duty of creating immortality, it now attains the right to kill, to become the murderer of the author. (117)

This brings us to the Structuralist-turned-Poststructuralist **Roland Barthes** (1915-80), who also points to the conventional father-figure of the author and pronounces him dead in his acclaimed essay "Death of the Author" (1967):

> We know now that a text is not a line of words releasing a single 'theological meaning' (the 'message' of the Author-God) but a multi-dimensional space in which a variety of writings, none of them original, blend and clash. The text is a tissue of quotations drawn from the innumerable centres of culture. (149)

This single comment at once points to different perceptions of author, text and the notion of originality. A text has plurality of meaning because rather than being the 'work' of the author, it is a blend of different texts already there. Barthes' book *S/Z* (1970) is a borderline case in that whereas Barthes presents a structuralist analysis of Balzac's story "Sarrasine", he also points out, in poststructuralist mode, that a text can never have a fixed meaning and a fixed structure. In his essay "From Work to Text", he states that the writer is the controller of his work; he is not the originator of the text. The meaning, according to him, lies with the reader, in inter-action with the text and it is only with the 'death' of the author that the reader is 'born'. Also a word about the notion of intertextuality should not be out of place here. Since the poststructuralists alienated the writing from the writer, the impersonal text is also found to be shorn of self-identity; it is intertextual being a function of language and culture. Different texts are not supposed to be really independent, rather they are joined and supported by a network of texts.

If text was under cloud, the reader too, was not spared. Most poststructural critics sharply criticize what they call 'humanism', —that the human being or author is a coherent identity and that he is endowed with purpose, initiative, etc. Instead of such traditional terms as 'human being', or 'individual' or 'self', post-structuralists tend to substitute **'subject'**. This is because this word is divested of the connotation that it is an originating or controlling power. Instead poststructuralists suggest that the human being is 'subjected to' the play of external forces, and it is also suggested by the grammatical term—the 'subject' of a sentence [Paul de Man: *Allegories of Reading* (1979)] which is an empty slot, to be filled in by whoever happens to be speaking at a particular time and place.

There is no doubt about it that deconstruction is at the root of poststructuralism. It has been instrumental in revision of theories which had been in vogue until then. Presently, **poststructuralist literary theories** can be divided into three categories: (1) those that are based on text or language, as for example, deconstruction; (2) those that are individual-oriented like psychoanalytic criticism, reader response theory and phenomenological approach; and (3) those which are society-oriented like marxian criticism, culture studies, feminist criticism, gender studies, postcolonial criticism, new historicism, queer theory, race studies, etc. All these theories have gained from the insight which Poststructuralism has provided to them.

In addition to the deconstructionists named above, the **Yale School followers** of Derrida must be mentioned for their contribution to the development of deconstruction. They are: Paul de Man, Geoffrey Hartman, J. Hillis Miller, Barbara Johnson and Harold Bloom. Among other leading poststructuralists, we can mention Jacques Lacan, Gilles Deleuze and Felix Guattari who have applied deconstruction to the field of psychology; Gayatri Chakravarti Spivak has used it to study the problems of Third World countries from the feminist angle. Other feminists of this denomination are Julia Kristeva and Luce Irigaray. Edward Said and Homi Bhabha have used this theory in the context of postcolonial societies. And of course Lyotard and Boudrillard, the high priests of postmodernism, are also poststructuralists.

Works Cited

Batra, Jagdish. *T.S. Eliot: A Deconstructive Reading.* New Delhi: Prestige, 2010.

Butler, Christopher. *Postmodernism.* Oxford: Oxford University Press, 2002.

Cuddon, J.A. *A Dictionary of Literary Terms and Literary Theory* (Fourth Edition). New Delhi: Maya Blackwell, 1998.

Derrida, Jacques. *Of Grammatology*, Johns Hopkins University Press, Baltimore, 1976.

———. *Margins of Philosophy.* Trans. Alan Bass. Sussex: Harvester, 1982.

Felperin, Howard. *Beyond Deconstruction: The Uses and Abuses of Literary Theory.* Oxford: Clarendon, 1985.

Habib, M.A.R. *A History of Literary Criticism.* Oxford: Blackwell Publishing, 2005, Indian Reprint, 2006.

Foucault, Michael. "The Order of Discourse". *Untying the Text*, Ed. Robert Young. Boston: Kegan Paul, 1981. pp. 48-78.

———. "What is an Author?" *Language, Counter-Memory, Practice: Selected Essays and Interviews*, Ed. And Trans. Donald F. Bouchard. New York: Cornell, 1977.

Ryan, Michael. *Literary Theory: A Practical Introduction* Massachussets: Blackwell, 1999, Reprint 2002.

Webster, Roger. *Studying Literary Theory: An Introduction* (Second Edition). London: Hodder Headline, 1996, Reprint 2001.

6

American Deconstruction/ Yale Critics

American critics experimented with a number of theories in their attempts to throw off the formalism of New Critics. The 'myth criticism' of Northrop Frye, the Hegelian Marxism of Lukacs, the phenomenology of Poulet, and French structuralism, each had its heyday. It is something of a surprise that Jacques Derrida won over many of America's most powerful critics. Derrida's greatest support has been the Department of English at Yale University. Paul de Man, Hillis Miller, Geoffrey Hartman, and Harold Bloom took to deconstruction in a major development for literary studies. The Yale School became synonymous with deconstruction in the 1970s.

Jacques Derrida (1930-2004), the spirit behind the poststructural movement of deconstruction, taught mainly in Europe—for about 24 years—and then in 1986, he joined the University of California where he stayed until shortly before his death. During this time, he was also associated as a visiting professor with a number of universities in America and Europe. So, he belonged as much to Europe as to the U.S.A. As Derrida's role in propounding and upholding the reading strategy (not a theory according to him) of deconstruction has been discussed in the chapter on 'Poststructuralism and Deconstruction', we move on to the American deconstrutionists inspired by Derrida, most of whom were working at the Yale School.

One of the most important members of the Yale School of Deconstruction was **Paul de Man** (1919-83). His *Blindness and Insight* (1971) and *Allegories of Reading* (1979) are impressive works of deconstruction. His debt to Derrida is evident, but de Man developed his own terminology. In his writings, he represented the basic conflicting forces within a text under the headings of grammar (the code or rules of language) as opposed to rhetoric (the unruly play of figures and tropes). He aligned these with other opposed forces such as the constantive and performative linguistic functions that had been distinguished by John Austin in his speech—act theory.

Paul de Man's *Blindness and Insight* revolves around the paradox that critics only achieve insight through a certain blindness. They adopt a method or theory which is quite different from what they meant to say. For example, the American New Critics based their practice upon the notion of organic form, according to which a poem has a formal unity. However, instead of discovering in poetry the unity and coherence, they reveal multi-faceted and ambiguous meanings. This contradicts the theory which they applied to interpret a poem.

In *Allegories of Reading*, de Man develops a **rhetorical type** of deconstruction. For de Man language is always figurative and not referential and there is no un-rhetorical language. Tropes or figures of speech allow the writer to say something and mean something different. Tropes destabilize logic and deny the possibility of a straightforward literal or referential use of language. De Man's famous example illustrates this. To the question tea or coffee, one replies, "What is the difference?" Here the actual and understood meaning is that it makes no difference if either tea or coffee is served. But this contradicts the logic of the literal meaning, which is: What is the difference between tea and coffee? Thus, the linguistic sign is merely the site of an ambivalent relationship between referential and figurative meaning.

For Paul de Man, reading is always a misreading because tropes constantly interfere between critical and literary texts. All types of language, whether used in economics, political theory, law, etc. work through metaphors just as any literary text does.

However, literature is the area where the irony and ambiguity between the literal and figurative is most visible. Paul de Man holds that any language in any text is rhetorical and figural, i.e. literary. Paul de Man's method of deconstruction is closest to Derrida's when he tries to show that a text's own rhetoric undermines what it tries to say. Here there is the *aporia*—an impasse, where there is the assertion and simultaneous negation of opposing systems of logic or rhetoric.

J. Hillis Miller (b. 1928) was formerly the leading representative of the Geneva School of Criticism known for promoting phenomenology in literary criticism. He later became one of the most prominent deconstructionists known especially for his application of this type of critical reading to prose fiction. His work since 1960 has centred on the deconstruction of fiction, especially in *Fiction and Repetition: Seven English Novels* (1982).

According to Miller, all signs are rhetorical figures and language is fictive. By going back to etymology, Miller disturbs the apparent meaning of the sign and opens out many more possibilities of interpretation. The reader is forced to move from one figure to another in an endless 'lateral dance'. Repetition and difference are favourite figures in fiction and repetition. For Miller, repetition means where everything repeats, but repeats differently. Analysing English novelists like Hardy and Dickens, Miller shows how a single figure or trope recurs in a text and with each recurrence appears different. Miller's aim is to show how all presence is based on difference and repetition.

In *Ardiane's Thread*, Miller uses the trope of lines—the linear progression of narratives, that is, line by line reading and physical arrangement of a text itself, the lines of physiognomy of characters, their family lines and genealogies, etc. to develop a whole series of deconstructive readings. Miller's conclusion is that any literary text is a play of irreconcilable and contradictory meanings. The text, is therefore, is indeterminable and undecidable. Therefore, all reading is necessarily misreading.

Having emerged from new criticism, **Geoffrey Hartman** (b. 1929) plunged into deconstruction and left a series of fragmentary texts which are collected in *Beyond Formalism*

(1970), *The Fate of Reading* (1975) and *Criticism in the Wilderness* (1980). He seeks a critical language that is highly figurative and critical at the same time. He has an eccentric style of writing that constantly calls attention to the manner of his own writing. Thus, erudition, vast scholarly references and clichés are present together in his work. According to Hartman, there are two extreme tendencies in modern criticism. The scholar critic relies too much on elucidation of texts. The philosopher-critic uses the text as a step in attaining absolute thinking. One has to bring these strands together and this is what deconstruction achieves.

Hartman argues that critical reading should not seek meaning but should reveal the contradictions in a text. The language of criticism must be as figurative, allusive and elusive as the poem it seeks to interpret. Hartman also rejects the death of the subject, and the idea of unlimited free-play. For Hartman, the Derridean notion of the completely undecidable is unacceptable. Interpretation, for him, is a consciousness of the self. This consciousness must be raised to critical heights. This self-reflective and self-conscious style has been Hartman's hallmark, most visible in his great book on Wordsworth.

In literary criticism, **Harold Bloom** (b. 1930) has made spectacular use of tropes. He treats literature as a special field of study. However, he combines his theory of tropes with Freudian psychology and cabbalistic mysticism (Jewish rabbinical texts which reveal hidden meanings in the Bible) as, for example, in his book *Shakespeare: The Invention of the Human*. Bloom is of the view that since Milton, English poets are aware of having arrived late in the poetic history, after many poetical fathers. These writers experience a certain Oedipal hatred of their father, and want to deny their paternity. They fear that their poetic fathers have already used up all the available inspiration. All poems must therefore be seen as written against the poetic father. This Bloom terms a 'misprision', a misreading of the past masters to produce a new interpretation. This intentional misreading creates the required space in which they can communicate their own authentic inspiration. There are three stages of revision in Bloom's psycho-poetics, namely limitation, or taking a new look; substitution, or replacing one form with another, and representation, or restoring a meaning. These are the stages through which a present poet passes when he tries to write something against the earlier poet. The 'anxiety of influence' is thus met through psychicdefences.

In *A Map of Misreading* (1975), Bloom shows how meaning is produced in 'Post-Enlightenment' images by the language strong poets use in defense against, and in response to, the language of prior strong poets. Bloom's work has thus sought to recast deconstructive readings within a 'historical rhetoric' (a term coined by Peter de Bolla) of poetic imagination and Freudian theory.

Gayatri Chakravorty Spivak (b. 1942), an American professor of Indian origin, caught the attention of the literary world through her translation of Derrida's *Of Grammotology* from French into English, but more than that for her scholarly introduction to this workcouched in a rather cumbersome prose. According to M.A.R. Habib, she is known for "her central concern with the structures of colonialism, the postcolonial subject, and the possibility of postcolonial discourse draws on deconstructive practices, the feminist movement, Marxism, and Freud" (747-48). Spivak has championed the cause of the Third World women and forcefully argued against clubbing them with the women of the developed world because of changes on the ground. In her famous essay "Can the Subaltern Speak?" (1983), she wondered if the subaltern could ever achieve a voice of his own.

Barbara Johnson analyses in *The Critical Difference* the networks of differences in both literary and critical texts. She deconstructs Roland Barthes' famous analysis of Balzac's Sarrasine, in which he applies the implications of his distinction between the 'readerly' and the 'writerly' texts. In her *A World of Difference*, Johnson applies deconstruction in the context of gender and racial differences. Similarly, Judith Butler, in *Gender Trouble: Feminism and the Subversion of Identity* (1990), deconstructs the question of identity for women and finds it unstable. Shoshana Fulman and Michael Ryan have studied psychoanalysis and Marxism respectively drawing inspiration from Derridean practice.

Going by what critics like Harold Bloom who has tried to deconstruct the poetic tradition, Barbara Johnson with her emphasis on gender and race and so on have done using deconstruction as a potent tool, one is apt to conclude that the purely semiological focus of deconstruction has gone astray. Even about Paul de Man's work it has been observed: "Raised through out de Man's work are questions of history, including the conditions of literary history and texts' impingement on historical events" (Chase, 254). This may be interpreted by some as expanding the bounds of deconstruction but there is no gainsaying that this certainly is a fallout and for this reason critics like Colin MacCabe, who talks about the "poverty with which Derrida's thought has been received in the US" (xv).

Seen against the historical context, the **point of difference** between American Deconstruction and Derridean Deconstruction was the fact that the American critics turned directly from phenomenology to deconstructive theory, skipping the structuralist phase, because structuralism and deconstruction arrived in America around the same time, i.e. in the late 1960s. At that time, some critics like Jonathan Culler and Robert Scholes turned to structuralism while others followed the path of deconstruction. Thus, American critics, especially those who were associated with the Yale University, made their contribution to Derrida's theory of deconstruction, though in their individual ways, but their allegiance to and dependence on Derrida cannot be negated.

Works Cited

Chase, Cynthia. "Paul de Man", *The John Hopkins Guide to Literary Theory & Criticism.* Second Edition. Eds. Groden, Michael et al. Baltimore: The John Hopkins University Press, 2005.

Habib, M.A.R. *A History of Literary Criticism.* Oxford: Blackwell Publishing, 2005, Indian Reprint, 2006.

MacCabe, Colin. "Foreword", In Other Worlds by Gayatri Chakravorty Spivak. New York: Routledge, 2006, Indian Reprint, 2012.

7

Postmodernism

Both modernism and postmodernism refer to philosophies of life which evolved due to economic and technological changes in the world. The **origin** of modernism lay in the loss of confidence in the Western world, whose claims of freedom and prosperity were proved to be hollow. The West continuously relied on Christian morals as bulwark against dissension and conflict but religion failed to deliver. Similarly, the economic philosophy of capitalism practised so far as a fool-proof path to prosperity created the categories of 'haves' and 'have-nots'. Even the democratic system failed to provide the happiness that comes with liberty; instead it created inept political structures. The beginning of modernism is taken anywhere from 1890s to the aftermath of First World War. In literature, it signifies the aesthetic tendencies associated mainly with writers like Eliot, Pound and Joyce. Modernism continued till 1960s, after which postmodernism made its presence felt.

Comparing the two further, it can be said that whereas modernism started with mass movement within the West, postmodernism started with mass migration from the East to the West. In postmodernism, we find that space, place, nation, etc. stand destabilized. Distinction between modernism and Postmodernism is blurred. One way is to look at the transformation of one into the other as a developing relationship "from a predominating concern with an apparent truthfulness or verisimilitude to an apparent reality, to a preoccupation with the forms in which a version of reality could be represented and a rejection of the conventions of realism, to an increasing conviction that it is not possible to represent reality at all—there is no sense of a unified or underlying reality" (Webster 123).

Another view is that there is no depth in postmodernism, only surface reality can be portrayed. The distinction beteen fact and fiction seems rather blurred. In a way, simulation as virtual reality is the norm in postmodern times, as for example, television characters are treated as real characters by the popular press and the big companies like the one running Disneyland would send actors in the guise of Micky Mouse or Spiderman on world tours so that people believe in the real existence of these characters.

The **first use** of the term 'Postmodernism' was made in 1947 by Charles Jenks with regard to architecture. According to Cuddon, the term 'Postmodernism' is used to refer to "changes, developments and tendencies which have taken place (and are taking place) in literature, art, music, architecture, philosophy, etc. since the 1940s or 1950s" (689). Some critics relate it to the transformation of European culture at the end of World War II. This war resulted in the use of dangerous weapons like the atom bomb and produced death camps, which represented the evil side of man in all its horrendousness and underlined the destructive potential of scientific knowledge and despotic regimes. The end of colonies and the post-war changes in the world economy and power structure also marked the beginning of a new era.

The intense debates and **theorization of postmodernism** took place in 1980s only. It was felt that postmodernism needs to be studied at three broad levels: firstly, in terms of the historical development, it designates the latest phase in the broad evolution of capitalist economics and culture that started in the later part of the twentieth century. The current phase dominated by multinational corporations thriving on mass media advertising and information technology is an extension of this kind of capitalism. Secondly, the term denotes psychological, social or political tendencies in that economics now moulds relationships, social structures and international political decisions. Thirdly, in the sphere of literary and cultural theory, the terms 'Postmodern' or 'Postmodernism' have been applied to the works of numerous writers such as Jacques Derrida, Michel Foucault, Julia Kristeva, etc. who have also been labelled 'poststructuralist'. Postmodernism is, in fact, a broader phenomenon; one of whose manifestations is poststructuralism.

The spirit of postmodernism, which found expression in art, architecture, music, film, literature, sociology, communications, fashion and other fields, was sought to be theorized by both Jean-Francois Lyotard (1924-98) and Jean Baudrillard (1929-2007). Lyolard's *The Postmodern Condition: A Report on Knowledge* has become something of a manifesto of postmodernism. It was a report prepared at the instance of the Quebec government. According to **Lyotard**, while realism was the pre-dominant style in literature of the eighteenth and nineteenth century, modernism emerged in late nineteenth century and continued to rule till World War II. Lyotard's writings are characterized by a persistent opposition to universals, meta-narratives as epitomized, for example, by Marxian and Freudian theories. He also vehemently criticized the so-called universalist claims of the Enlightenment.

> Lyotard argues that the 'great narratives' that underpin Western civilization—religion, Marxism, the idea of progress through the application of rational principles, the belief that a completely free market will ultimately benefit us all—have at least theoretically been discredited. All those 'metanarratives' are guilty of having declared themselves universally valid and they have all contributed to the West's oppression, if not actual enslavement, of a good deal of the world. (Bertnes 142-43)

Building upon what he calls the 'theological' underpinnings of both Freud and Marx, Lyotard seeks to define postmodernism as an extension of modernism but with a different focus:

> The Postmodern would be that which, in the moderns puts forward the unpresentable in presentation itself; that which denies itself the solace of good forms, the consensus of a taste which would make it possible to share presentations, not in order to enjoy them but in order to impart a stronger sense of the unrpresentablc. (81)

Thus, whereas modernism suffers from the nostalgia of the aesthetic of sublime and yet tries unsuccessfully to present this unpresentable, postmodernism has no nostalgia and tries to find new presentations not in order to enjoy them but just to convey the idea that it is still unpresentable. All the same, whereas loss marks the modernist sentiment, there is excitement writ large in postmodernism with regard to this issue of representation. Postmodernism borrows from modernism, the disillusionment with the 'givens' or the accepted norms/beliefs of society, fragmentation and ambiguity, a decentered and deconstructed subject, etc. But while modernism saw this fragmentation (as in Eliot's *The Waste Land*) as tragic, postmodernism, on the other hand, celebrates the activity of fragmentation. Whereas modernism still seeks a rational meaning in a work of art, postmodernism explores the irrationality of art.

The other theoretician **Baudrillard** is fascinated by the 'simulacra' of postmodern life which have taken the place of real objects. In fact, the simulacrum becomes reality itself. The simulacrum is the copy that is so close to the original that the original is no longer important. Think, for example, of video or music compact discs, for which there is no original the way one might look for original paintings or statues. Virtual reality games add another dimension to the artificiality of modern life. Reality TV becomes the 'actual' reality for us. Thus, with the death of the 'real', the 'hyper-real' takes over.

Broadly speaking, we can perhaps identify three **salient features** which differentiate postmodern literature from modern literature. Firstly, postmodernism—in both subject matter and style—is marked by recognition of ethnic, sexual and cultural diversity. Whereas modernist texts work from the outside, postmodernist works tend to give the other a voice—to analyze cultural difference from within. Secondly, whereas high modernism (with exceptions such as Brecht) prided itself on highbrow status and learned allusions, postmodernism deliberately extends into the domain of popular culture. For it, there is no hierarchy of high/low culture. Finally, there is a difference of motive. Whereas postmodernist writing exhibits difference, diversity, incoherence and a world of surfaces and there is no attempt to give them a unified identity, in modernism, difference is still included in identity as is experimentation in tradition. For example, T.S. Eliot's *The Waste Land*, which expresses a fragmented world, relies heavily on allusions which point to a unity in traditional forms of life. On the other hand, Beckett's *Waiting for Godot*, which is now considered postmodernist, exhibits no structure in its allusions. The action of the play defies every category of action and its location is entirely abstract and unidentifiable.

In brief, postmodernism **stands for freedom** from tradition and authority. No centre, definite terms, boundaries or absolute truths exist. Truth is relative and subjective. The margins are as important as the centre. It stands for the contingent, the subversive and the functional. Irreverence towards authority, indeterminacy, experiments in techniques, eclecticism, pastiche, magic realism, collapse of demarcation between fact and fiction, non-recognition of boundaries, belief in relativity of critical approaches are some of the other hallmarks of postmodern literature. What postmodernism challenges are old style liberalism, its high moral tone with tradition and its high attendant notions of purity and authenticity considered implicit in the conventional forms of social life. What postmodernism celebratesare differences, diversity, eccentricity, novelty, hybridism—in a way—irrevocable splitting of the sign into signifier and signified, etc. Postmodernism thus reflects the energy and diversity of contemporary life as well as its frequent lack of coherence and depth.

Ihab Hassan (91-92) has worked out the differences between the two movements; some of which are as follows:

	Modernism	Postmodernism
1.	Form (conjunctive/closed)	Anti-form (disjunctive/ open)
2.	Purpose	Play
3.	Design	Chance
4.	Hierarchy	Anarchy
5.	Art object/Finished Work	Process/Performance/ Happening
6.	Presence	Absence
7.	Centering	Dispersal
8.	Genre/Boundry	Text/Intertext
9.	Root/Depth	Rhizome/Surface
10.	Lisible (Readerly)	Scriptible/Writerly

The lack of clarity regarding the distinction between modernism and postmodernism is reflected in borderline cases like Samuel Beckett who was earlier regarded as a modernist but is now hailed as a great postmodernist. Postmodern literature is marked by a **complex combination** of techniques, genres and discourses. We also find a return to the pleasure principle and representationalism. So, pop art and pastiche find favour with the postmodernists. As an example, we can take up John Fowles' *The French Lieutenant's Woman* (1969), which combines passages from Darwin, Marx, Arnold, etc. quotations from sociological reports, frequent authorial comments as also his own transmutation as a character in the novel, which is couched in a typical 19th century narrative form. A very significant literary piece *Midnight's Children* written by Salman Rushdie employs a mélange of literary devices like magic realism, irony, symbolism, allusions and a ubiquitous word-play based on puns and startling coinages. The protagonist Saleem Sinai is one of the 1001 children born at the stroke of midnight when India became free and all these children have magical telepathic powers. Four hundred and twenty children die later. Saleem is said to be irretrievably chained to history of India and his self is constituted by the contests and conflicts of history. His crisis of identity is seen to represent the crisis of the nation at the time of independence. The narrative is an allegory of the developments in the life of India and Pakistan. In this, Rushdie has sought to re-write history. Often such postmodern texts are found to be self-reflexive in nature.

It would be apt to remark that the **fascination for history**, mostly current, has inspired postmodern writing from Gunther Grass to Salman Rushdie and the march continues. Wartime experience has been at the back of many such attempts. Apart from it, the question of identity has assumed great significance in our times. As the world became a global village, the notion of nation and nationality required a fresh look. One finds this issue addressed artistically in Amitav Ghosh's *The Shadow Lines*. Ethnicity, environment, feminism are some other important perspectives found in postmodern literature. Racism has been effectively taken up by American writers Alice Walker and Tony Morrison.

So far as the scenario of criticism is concerned, we find **hybridism** reflected here. Roland Barthes' *S/Z* (1974) falls in the category of 'creative criticism' of Balzac's novella *Sarrasine* in the sense that he extends the boundaries of criticism also while reviewing this work. Barthes' real interest lies in the numerous digressions, whimsical punctuation and capitalization and, for what was found unique in him as a critic—fictive elements. Similar is the case of Julian Barnes' criticism of Flaubert's life and works. In this kind of criticism, a medley of techniques have been employed. It is not pure; it is highly inter-disciplinary.

The **opponents** of postmodernism have included notably left-wing intellectuals such as Jurgen Habermas, Frederic Jameson, and Terry Eagleton. According to Frederic Jameson, artistic movements like modernism and postmodernism are cultural formations that accompany particular stages of capitalism and are to some extent constructed by it. Not all agree with Lyotard's formulation of postmodernism as the negation of all grand narratives, as Chrstipher Butler remarks,

"The general sociological claim that such narratives are in decline in our period looks pretty thin, even after the collapse of state-sponsored Marxism in the West" (14). This is because allegiances to large-scale, totalizing religious and nationalist beliefs are currently responsible for so much repression, violence and war—in Northern Ireland, Serbia, the Middle East, for instance. Postmodernists tend not to be well informed about current practices in science and religion. It is obvious to any reader of the newspapers that men and women are still more or less willing to kill one another in the name of grand narratives—think of the *fatwa* against Salman Rushdie.

Works Cited

Bertnes, Hans. *Literary Theory: The Basics*. Oxford: Routledge, 2001.

Cuddon, J.A. *A Dictionary of Literary Terms and Literary Theory* (Fourth Edition). New Delhi: Maya Blackwell, 1998.

Webster, Roger. *Studying Literary Theory: An Introduction* (Second Edition). London: Hodder Headline, 1996, Reprint 2001.

Christopher Butler. *Postmodernism*. Oxford: Oxford University Press, 2002.

Hasan, Ihab. *The Postmodern Turn: Essays in Postmodern Theory and Culture*. Ohio: Ohio State University, 1987.

Lyotard, Jean Francois. "Answering the question: What is Postmodernism?" in *The Postmodern Condition*. Minnesota, U.S.: University of Minnesota Press, 1979 tr. 1984.

8

Marxist Criticism

Marxism has been one of the most influential intellectual movements in the history of ideas. Its influence can be seen in many fields—history, cultural studies, economics, psychoanalysis, sociology, cultural theory, etc. Marxist theory begins in the massive work of Karl Marx (1818-83) and Friedrich Engels (1820-95) in the 19th century. Their writings mainly deal with the discipline of economics and politics. However, their analysis of society and the conditions of production affect analysis of culture also. And this is the significance of Marx as also of the later-day Marxist critics and thinkers.

Marxist approaches to literature occupy a wide field and have diverse forms. The theory and practice of Marxist criticism is based on the economic and cultural theory of Karl Marx and his fellow-thinker Engels. The theory claims that the evolving history of humanity, of its social institutions, and of its ways of thinking are largely determined by the changing **mode of material** production, that is, its overall economic ogranisation for producing and distributing material goods. Changes in the fundamental mode of material production bring about changes in the class structure of a society. This results in establishing dominant and subordinate classes. These classes engage in a struggle for economic, political, and social advantage. The Marxists maintain that human consciousness is constituted by an ideology. By 'ideology', they mean the beliefs, values, and ways of thinking and feeling through which they perceive and explain what they take to be reality.

In literature, the main focus of Marxist criticism was **the novel**, especially the 19th century novel. Marx concentrated his economics and social analysis on this period. He was himself an avid reader of Charles Dickens in particular. The concerns of Marxist critics generally have been primarily social rather than individual. They explore the sociology of the text as opposed to the psychology of individual characters. When characters are examined, it is usually as a way of exploring the wider social and historical forces of which they are seen as products. Significant developments in Marxist literary criticism took place in the 1920s and 1930s. They centred largely on the issue of realism.

The doctrines expounded by the Union of Soviet writers (1932-34) were based upon Lenin's pre-Revolutionary statements as interpreted during the 1920s. They constitute what is called **Socialist Realism**. The theory addressed certain major questions about the evolution of literature, its reflection of class relations, and its function in society. The revolutions in European art, music, and literature around 1910 (Picasso, Starvinsky, T.S. Eliot, etc.) were to be regarded by Soviet critics as decadent products of late capitalist society. The modernist rejection of traditional realism left Socialist Realism as the leading custodian of bourgeois aesthetics. The combination of nineteenth-century aesthetics and revolutionary politics remained the focus of this theory. According to Raman Seldon, "The theory of the class nature of art (*klassovost*) is a complex one. In the writings of Marx, Engels and the Soviet tradition, there is a double emphasis on the writer's commitment or class interests on the one hand, and the social realism of the writer's work on the other" (27). So, the writers are judged by the extent to which their writings reveal insights into the social developments of their time.

The early twentieth century Marxism criticism as evidenced in several **books** is a reflective one. British Marxist Christopher Caudwell, in his *Illusion and Reality* (1937), discusses English poets like Mathew Arnold, Swinburne, Browning and Tennyson and finds them reflecting only bourgeois illusion. In the Soviet Union also, a number of critics like Mikhail Bakhtin tried to combine Marxist theory with Russian Formalism. Bakhtin collaborated with P.N. Medvedev to produce *The Formal Method in Literary Scholarship* (1928), and also wrote Marxism and the Philosophy of Language (1929) with Valentin Voloshinov. In these works, they sought to evolve, what they called 'sociological poetics'. These attempts were not very successful and ended in fiasco when the Russian strongman Stalin took over power.

The best known and probably most influential critic here is the Hungarian **Georg Lukacs** (1885-1971). His work concentrated mainly on the nineteenth century novel and questions of realism. "For Lukacs, as with most Marxist critics of his time", says Roger Webster, "a novel must be assessed on its ability to reflect the historical and material conditions of society" (68). These were the main criteria of assessing its realism. Ralph Fox's work, *The Novel and the People* (1937), is a good example of an English Marxist critic working along similar lines in the same period. Realism was not related to the ability of the text to show surface reality, rather the point to be marked was the extent to which the sense of the underlying historical relations were depicted, and if it conveyed the totality of a Marxist vision of history. Lukac's concept of 'typicality' was not the average representation of a character, rather it was when the objective forces at work in society were shown to determine his innermost being. Thus, Lukacs is concerned with the way the characters are shown a part of a total social and historical fabric. Lukacs and other Marxists rejected the subjective and the experimental nature of much modernist writing. He felt that such works deal with individuals rather than the more 'objective' vision. Marxist critics have not all been opposed to experimentation.

Two Marxist **writers of the 1930s** developed critical practices which offer a very different approach to literature from that typified by Lukacs. The dramatist Bertolt Brecht introduced the concept of defamiliarization by breaking with the conventions of theatrical realism. The term for this technique was the 'alienation effect'. The work of German critic Walter Benjamin, who was a staunch supporter of Brecht, is very significant. He argued that the technical revolution of the early 20th century in terms of the media and mass circulation of books of all kinds enabled everybody to be an artist. This was because the means of expression were becoming easily available. He saw the artist not as someone producing a detached reflection of reality but something that was integral to reality. Thus, his sympathy towards modernism is quite evident in a period when most of the Marxist thinkers condemned it.

The **Frankfurt School**, which was the other name for the Institute for Social Research, was founded by Carl Grunberg in 1923. It was the first Marxist research centre associated with a major German university. The leading figures of this school are Theodor Adorno, Max Horkheimer and Herbert Marcuse. They opposed Benjamin's ideas about the mass circulation of art. They dismissed realism as reinforcing conventional ways of thinking. The kind of literature for which they argued was one that expressed a detachment from reality. Adorno's conception of art, in particular, is quite different. He stresses the need to go beyond what is palatable to the masses. The Italian critic **Antonio Gramsci** (1891-1937) has adopted certain fundamental categories for his analysis of culture and society. He has used terms like instrumentalism, reductionism, ideology, hegemony, etc. He is against traditional Marxist theory. According to Gramsci, literature participates for hegemony in society. It may help oppose oppressive hegemony by suggesting and popularizing new types of hegemony.

The French critic **Pierre Macherey** (b. 1938) combined Marxism with structuralism in his *A Theory of Literary Production* which though published in 1966, was translated into English only in 1978. He believed that form cannot be separated from ideology, because a literary work is limited by time and space and it cannot be free from the historical reality to which it is tied in complex ways. History is not directly to be grasped in literature. To do so, one has to access the 'unconscious' of literature and the job of a critic is to grasp history in a text in its gaps, fissures or absences. There is no order in a text but an imagined one. For these analogies, Macherey is indebted to Freudian psychology.

The French Marxist **Louis Althussar** (1918-90) was another theorist who gave a new direction to Marxism. He views literature generally as performing a rather ambiguous function. It acts as a form of ideology, blinding people to their real conditions of existence. It is also capable of detaching itself from the very ideology in which it participates. According to Althussar, some literature reinforces the dominant values, some questions them, and some does both. His work *Lenin and Philosophy and Other Essays* (1971), which is a collection of essays, had a great impact on critical thinking of the time. His ideas were responsible for the break with the old reflective model of Marxist criticism. Besides, he substituted the concept of 'social formation' for the Marxist notion of 'totality'. The social formation is a structure with various levels and is without any fixed centre; it is a totality but in it is the economic level that determines other structures and levels. Various elements of the social formation are legal, religious, educational and cultural which he calls 'ideological state apparatuses'. He also did not agree with the Marxist view of ideology as being a 'false consciousness'. Instead, it was defined as the imaginary relationship of individuals to their real conditions of existence.

Two British critics who have perhaps contributed most to recent Marxist theory are Terry Eagleton and Fredric Jameson. **Fredric Jameson** (b. 1934) views Marxism as the only antidote to the advance of Western monopolistic capitalism. According to Jameson, literature works as a form of ideological discourse which represses historical truth. In his *The Political Unconscious* (1981), he tries a reconciliation of the types of Marxism propounded by Lukcas and Althusser respectively. This inclusivist formulation also envelopes non-Marxist critical approaches like formalism, structuralism and poststructuralism. About this concept, Satya Mohanty comments that the political unconscious demonstrates that "textual meaning is not simply discovered; it is produced in a mediated way. Interpretation is, for Jameson...an opening up of the text to the winds of history" (qtd. Roberts, 96). "Apart from it, Jameson advances the concept of 'political unconscious', which is the function of history as it is inalienable from politics."

Terry Eagleton's (b. 1943) position is rather different from that of Althusser, and other Marxists. According to him, "Marxist criticism is not merely a 'sociology of literature', concerned with how novels get published and whether they mention the working class. Its aim is to explain the literary work more fully; and this means a sensitive attention to its forms, styles and meanings. But it also means grasping those forms, styles and meanings as the product of a particular history (23). Besides, ideology for him becomes a much more complex area than some Marxists think. Eagleton views the novel as ultimately reinforcing the status quo through its complex strategies. He argues for a re-conception of literature by changing the ways in which literature is constructed as a body of culture and knowledge. He does not agree to the negativistic view that history has gaps and absences. He modifies it to mean that history is present in the text as ideology and the reality claimed to be present in the text is only 'pseudo reality'.

It might be supposed that the Marxist literary criticism would have become an anachronism in a world turning toward market capitalism. In fact, however, Marxist criticism has not disappeared as a critic sums up, "There has been much talk in recent years about the 'demise of Marxism'.... No, far from consigning the Marxist project to the scrap-heap, the collapse of state socialism...creates both a need and an opportunity: the need to re-engage with the historical materiality, the 'real relations', of a world in bad trouble, and the opportunity to do so once again in the open air, free from the overbearing presence of a monopolized Marxist orthodoxy that blighted everything in its shade" (Davies, 149-50). The Marxist approach has actually thrived in the West in the form of a critique, a discourse for interrogating all societies and their texts in terms of certain specific issues—race, class, culture, etc. Marxist criticism is an important area of theoretical work and a significant contrast to other critical approaches.

Works Cited

Davies, Tony: "Marxist Aesthetics", *Literary Theory and Criticism*. Ed. Patricia Waugh. Oxford: Oxford University Press, 2006, Third Impression, 2009, pp. 140-51.

Eagleton, Terry, *Marxism and Literary Criticism*, London: Routledge, 2002.

Roberts, Adam. *Fredric Jameson*. London: Routledge, 2007.

Selden, Raman. *A Reader's Guide to Contemporary Literary Theory*. Sussex: Harvester, 1985.

9

Psychoanalytic Criticism

Psychoanalytic criticism is defined as "a form of literary criticism which uses some of the techniques of psychoanalysis in the interpretation of literature. Psychoanalysis itself is a form of therapy which aims to cure mental disorders by investigating the interaction of conscious and unconscious elements in the mind" (Barry, 96). The former seeks to unravel the latent content or the 'subtext' of a work by identifying fantasies, fears and desires. The two great theorists of this school are Sigmund Freud (1856-1939) and Jacques Lacan (1901-81). While many systems have been used to understand human psychology, the most influential in literary criticism in the twentieth century has been the one developed by Freud and his followers like Ernest Jones and Marie Bonaparte and expounded and related more closely to the theory of literature by Lacan.

Freud's concepts have often caused **controversy**. So, his theories continue to be reviewed, refined, revised, and even rejected. In recent years, many psychologists and literary scholars have debated how tainted Freudian psychology shows gender bias, while some of his concepts like 'penis envy' and 'phallic phase' establish a male normative base. No wonder then that some scholars have emphatically rejected Freud's approach to psychology because of its overmuch focus on sexuality.

The foundation of Freud's contribution to modern psychology is his **emphasis on the unconscious** aspects of the human psyche. He believed that most of our actions are motivated by psychological forces over which we have very little control. He demonstrated that human mind is structured in a way that its major portion is below the level of consciousness. In *The Anatomy of the Mental Personality*, Freud shows the difference between the levels of conscious and unconscious mental activity. He comments that we call a process "unconscious" when we have to assume that it was active at a certain time, although at that time we knew nothing about it. Freud defines two kinds of unconscious: the unconscious which is transformed into conscious material easily and another in the case of which such a transformation is difficult.

Freud's major premise is that most of the individual's processes are unconscious. The second premise is that all human behaviour is motivated by what we call sexuality. This, however, has been rejected by many professional psychologists, including some of Freud's own disciples—for example, Carl Gustav Jung and Alfred Adler. According to Freud, the prime psychic force is *libido*, or sexual energy. His third major premise is that because of powerful social taboos attached to certain sexual impulses, many of our desires and memories are repressed, which means, they are actively excluded from our consciousness.

Further, Freud divides mental processes into three psychic zones: the *id*, the *ego*, and the *superego*. The diagram appearing on page 63 illustrates the point.

The diagram helps to clarify the relationship between **id, ego** and **super-ego,** and also their collective relationship to the conscious and the unconscious. We should note that *id* is entirely unconscious. The *id* is the reservoir of *libido*, the primary source of all psychic energy. It functions to fulfil the primordial life principle, which Freud considers to be the pleasure principle. "Naturally, the *id* knows no values, no good, no evil, no morality," says he in his essay 'The Structure of the Unconscious (1940). In short, the *id* is the source of all our aggressions and desires. It is lawless, asocial and amoral. Its function is to gratify our instincts for pleasure without regard to social conventions or moral restraint. The *id* as defined by Freud as identical in many respects to the Devil as defined by theologians.

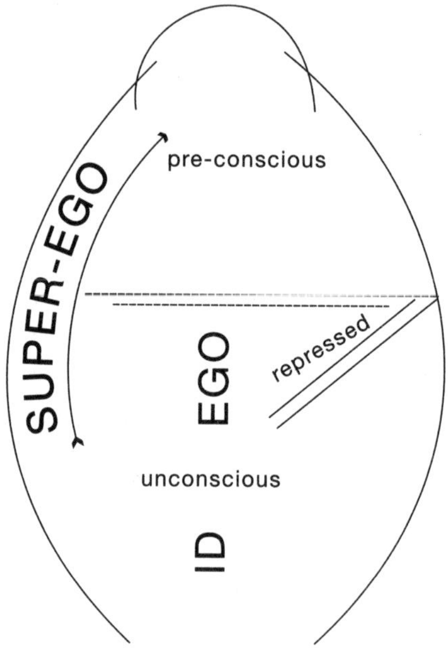

The ego is the regulating agency which protects the individual from the dangers posed by the *id*. This is the rational governing agent of the psyche. Though a large portion of the *ego* is unconscious, even then the *ego* comprises what we think of as the conscious mind. The *ego* stands for good reason and good sense, while the *id* stands for the untamed passions. While *id* is governed by the pleasure principle, the *ego* is governed by the reality principle.

The other regulating agent which functions to protect society is the *superego*. It is the repository of conscience and pride. It is the representative of all moral restrictions, the 'higher' things in human life. It serves to control the drives of the *id*. Whereas the *id* is dominated by the pleasure principle and the *ego* by the reality principle, the superego is dominated by the morality principle. We might say the *id* would make us devils, the *ego* healthy and rational human beings and the *superego* would make us angels.

Many scholars do not accept Freud's three-fold division of the psyche. But they have not reacted against the application of his theories to the symbolic interpretation of literature. However, the most controversial point of psychoanalytical criticism is its tendency to interpret **imagery** in terms of sexuality. The psychoanalytic critic tends to interpret all concave images (ponds, cups, caves, etc.) as female symbols. All images whose length exceeds their diameter (towers, mountain peaks, snakes, knives, swords, etc.) are male or phallic symbols. Perhaps even more objectionable is the interpretation of such activities as dancing, riding and flying as symbols of sexual pleasure.

Even more controversial than Freudian dream symbolism are Freud's theories concerning **child psychology**. Contrary to traditional beliefs, Freud found infancy and childhood as periods of intense sexual experience. During the first five years of life, the child passes through a series of phases in erotic development. Each phase is marked by emphasis on a particular portion of the body in which the sexual pleasure becomes localized. Freud indicated three such zones: the oral, the anal, and the genital. These zones are associated not only with pleasure in stimulation but also with the gratification of our vital needs like eating and reproduction. If the individual is frustrated while seeking to gratify these needs during childhood, the development of his personality may be arrested.

According to Freud, the child reaches the stage of genital primacy when he is five years old. It is the time when Oedipus complex manifests itself. The Oedipus complex derives from the boy's unconscious rivalry with his father for the love of his mother. Freud borrowed the term from the classic Sophoclean Tragedy *Oedipus, the King*. In this tragedy, the hero unwillingly murders his father and marries his mother.

Freud's theories have been applied to the **interpretation** of some literary works like Shakespeare's play Hamlet, and Herman Melville's *Moby Dick*. In *Hamlet*, King Claudius represents Hamlet's repressed hostility toward his father as a rival for his mother's affection. In *Moby Dick*, the White Whale represents the strict conscience (*superego*) of New England Puritanism. Captain Ahab, the monomaniac, who leads the crew of Pequod is interpreted as the symbol of uncontrollable *id*. Starbuck, the sane Christian, symbolizes a balanced and sensible rationalism ego.

However, there has been a widespreadmistrust of the psychological approach as a tool for critical analyses. Conservative scholars and teachers of literature are often shocked by the sexual terms used in this approach. The followers of Freudian approach lose sight of the thematic and aesthetic considerations. Some critics of this school use a lot of jargon which sometimes becomes difficult to understand. Then many critics of the psychological school have been literary scholars who have understood this theory imperfectly and professional psychologists who have had little feeling for literature as art.

Freud's disciple **Jacques Lacan** (1901-1981), also called "the French Freud", developed a semiotic version of Freudian psychology. He is certainly the most influential psychoanalytic thinker since Freud. He converted the basic concepts of psychoanalysis in the light of linguistic theory of Ferdinand de Saussure. Lacan always claimed that he was developing and formalizing ideas on which Sigmund Freud had worked. Freud propounded the discipline of psychoanalysis, which has two closely related aspects: clinical work and academic work. Clinical work is carried out with patients who suffer from psychological problems. Academic psychoanalysis aims to study the mental life in general and includes the study of literature and social sciences.

According of Lacan, the practice of psychoanalysis is dependent exclusively on words, which means on language. So psychoanalysis must have a theory of its language and meaning. The Surrealists showed that one image can be associated with more than one meaning. But Freud and Lacan claim that meaning has essentially to do with words, language, and symbols. But whereas Freud studied the relationship between biology and mind, Lacan studied culture, language and mental structure. Whereas Freud sets up a three-fold division of the mind—the *id*, the *ego*, and the *superego*, Lacan creates a trilogy of the *imaginary*, *the symbolic* andsometimes, *the real*. The first stage is the imaginary in which, according to M.H. Abrams, "there is no clear distinction between the subject and the object, or between the individual self and other selves" (251).

In the pre-Oedipal stage, the child has a symbiotic relationship with the mother and does not distinguish between itself and the mother's body. Lacan agrees with Freud that the **infant world** provides the basis for later identity. The fantasies and experiences of infantile consciousness are produced in the human subject through language. For Lacan, one does not live in a world of realities, but a world of signs, of signifiers. When he says that the unconscious is structured like a language, he means that the unconscious works through metaphors and signs. In other words, unconscious desires are revealed through free associations and dreams. Just as language operates as a system, in the same way society also operates through a series of interrelated signs, roles and rituals. This order he called the Symbolic Order.

Further the child has to repress his desire for the mother. The desire now goes into the unconscious. This new order is the symbolic, the law and order of the father. So language is the symbolic order, which constitutes the universe of the child. In its entry into the symbolic, the child is made aware of the sexual difference, the recognition of the phallus and gender role. This leads to the child's socialization. The male child enters language and the symbolic order after resolving the Oedipal crisis. In so doing it identifies with the father, the patriarchal order of the phallus. For Lacan, the phallus is the primary signifier, the place of power in language, through which the symbolic order is imposed.

The next stage is the **Mirror Stage** that spans the ages of six and eighteen months. The infant now learns to identify with its image in a mirror—the Other, and begins to develop a sense of a separate self and an understanding of itself as an autonomous subject, or an ideal *ego*, a perfect and unified self. By doing this, according to Lacan, it imagines a self that has no lack, no notion of absence, insufficiency or incompleteness. But this is simply an illusion. This is because our 'identity' or 'subjectivity' is construed in our interaction with others, the individuals who resemble us in one way or another, but who are different. We become ourselves by way of other perspectives and other's views of who we are. Since others' views are subject to change, identity is not stable and fixed; it is a process that can never lead to completion. Identity is not only subject to constant change, it can also be never coherent. This is because different people have different notions of us. Besides this, when we enter the realm of language, identity can be said to be a linguistic construct because subjectivity is constructed in language.

With the mirror stage, the child enters the language system. The figure of the father, prohibitions and laws also enter the child's world. For a child, the father is the Law. Social taboos are instilled in the child in the prohibition of incest. The child discovers that it is separate from the mother. It is a part of family and society in which it is expected to play a specific part. It discovers that identity is based on difference—its difference from others.

If the Imaginary is the domain of images and the Symbolic that of signifiers, **the Real**, in Lacan's theory, is beyond both. It cannot be imagined, symbolized or known directly. For Lacan, the real is that which resists representation. It constantly eludes our efforts to name it. So it challenges both the imaginary and the symbolic. The Real is not the 'objective world'; it is something 'impossible to say', or 'impossible to imagine' as Lacan says.

Lacan's development of Freud has had several important **influences**. Some feminists have suggested the social and political relationships between males and females will not change unless language itself has been radically changed. Second, Lacan's theory has proved of interest to deconstructors and other poststructuralists. This is because it holds that the ego is a product or construct. It is produced during the mirror stage and seems unified. But, according to Lacan, the unified self or *ego* is a fiction. So it is the job of the Lacan psychoanalyst to 'deconstruct' the *ego* to show contradictions in it.

Psychoanalytic Theory has permeated the postmodern condition. It has impacted many areas like historiography, feminism, film studies and Poststructuralism on the whole. While feminist critics like Luce Irigaray, Helene Cixous, Judith Butler and Juliet Mitchell have applied Lacanian psychoanalysis to their readings of texts in complex ways, the work of the versatile duo **Gilles Deleuzeand** and **Felix Guattari** stands out as they have extended the bounds of psychoanalysis. Commenting on their work, Sharla Hutchison et al. aver that they "seek to critique psychoanalysis in order to transform it altogether, ultimately to destroy it by unmasking its ideological foundation in the values of bourgeois culture" (785).

Deleuze and Guatttari came up with the concept of '**schizoanalysis**'. In *Anti-Oedipus* (1977), they reject the idea of repression and point out that trying to create an ego in a schizoid or a person with lack of interest in social relationships can lead to sickness. This is because the unconscious if forced to enter the domain of signifiers, even though it is already full of its own reservoir of images. This was opposed to Lacan's formulation that the unconscious is all about a lack or vacuity. Lack, according to Deleuze and Guattari, is created by the contemporary market forces which always impel one to absorb one image or the other—buy this or that product from the market because one is persuaded to believe that s/he does not have it and thereby has a 'lack'. They remark: "Schizophrenia is the exterior limit of capitalism itself or the conclusion of its deepest tendency, but that capitalism only functions on condition that it inhibits this tendency, or that it pushes back or displaces this limit" (qtd. Nayar, 81). The terms for such schizoids used by them are 'orphans' or 'nomads', because, as they point out, desire is personal but the collective in the midst of which the individual lives, is law. To overcome the antipathy involved, they propose the concept of 'social desire'. In their work *A Thousand Plateaus* (1987), Deleuze and Guattari criticized the central organ model of the unconscious in the form of a tree and instead came up with the 'rhizome' model represented by grass-type growth, with its multiple beginnings and endings—quite a different version of the unconscious. Thus, the deviation from Freud and Lacan in the work of Deleuze and Guattari has been instrumental in extending the scope of psychoanalysis.

Works Cited

Abrams, M.H. and Geoffrey Galt Harpham. *A Handbook of Literary Terms*. New Delhi: Cengage Learning, 2009.

Barry, Peter. *Beginning Theory: An Introduction to Literary and Cultural Theory*. Manchester, UK: Manchester University Press, 1999.

Hutchison, Sharla et al. 'Psychoanalytic Theory and Criticism'. *The John Hopkins Guide to Literary Theory & Criticism*. Second Edition. Eds. Groden, Michael et al. Baltimore: The John Hopkins University Press, 2005.

Nayar, Pramod. *Contemporary Literary and Cultural Theory: From Structuralism to Ecocriticism*. New Delhi: Longman, 2011.

10

Archetypal and Myth Criticism

The term 'myth' has in the Greek word 'mythos', which means a story. Myth normally refers to the ancient tales, mostly of heroism, romance and war, which different races have cherished over the ages. These are the symbolic projections of a people's hopes, values, fears, and aspirations. Myth can be defined as "a complex of stories—some no doubt fact and some fantasy—which for various reasons, human beings regard as demonstrations of the inner meaning of the universe and of human life" (Watts, 7). Myths are collective and communal productions, which serve the purpose of binding a tribe or a nation together. Myth is a found everywhere in human society. It transcends time and unites the past and present of any cultural collective. Every culture has its own distinctive mythology which is reflected in legends, anecdotes and even the thinking of the group. Myths take their specific form from the cultural environments in which they grow. Moreover, similar motifs may be found in different myths. Certain images that recur in the myths of people widely separated in time and place tend to have a common meaning.

Mythological approach to literature, also called **Myth Criticism,** had its roots in the psychological study of Sigmund Freud (1856-1939). While Myth Criticism grew as a reaction to the New Criticism, its objective was not to evolve into a critical approach, rather it studied the relationship between myths and literature. Some scholars have labored over finding the link between myths and history also. The contribution of the anthropologist James Frazer (1854-1941) too cannot be denied as he studied myths of different nations and brought out commonalities. The structuralist anthropologist Claude Levi Strauss (1908-2009) discovered that "the meaning of myth lies not in their manifest content but rather in their underlying structure of relations, which typically works to mediate between polar extremes (raw and cooked, agriculture and warfare, life and death). In other words, the purpose of myth is to provide a logical model capable of overcoming a contradiction" (Reeves, 674). Thus, myths override the causal nexus but they appeal to some deeper human faculty.

While anthropology was at the root of myth criticism, analytical psychology formed the basis of **archetypal criticism**. Carl Gustav Jung's (1875-1961) theory of depth psychology divides the psyche into three parts. The first is ego, which Jung identifies with the conscious mind. Closely related is the *personal unconscious*, which includes anything which is not presently conscious, but can be. The third is the *collective unconscious* that manifests itself in dreams, myths, and literature through archetypes. The archetypes are persistent images, figures, and story patterns shared by people of different cultures. Archetypal criticism was also influenced by the studies of a group of Cambridge University anthropologists. They found that certain myths and rituals recurred in a wide variety of cultures. Such motifs and images are called archetypes. In Greek language from which the term is derived, 'arche' stands for beginning and 'typos' for image or impression. So, these are the primordial or primary impressions carried by humans in their unconscious selves. In simple words, archetypes are universal symbols.

It should be understood that the disciplines of psychology and anthropology meet at some point. So far as Freud is concerned, he did not merely study the individual levels of human psychology or its clinical study as Geurin at all points out, "Sigmund Freud ranged far beyond experimental and clinical study into the realms of myth, and his distinguished sometime protégé, Jung became one of the foremost mythologists of our time"

(183). There is no doubt that while psychoanalysis deals with individual personality, myths deal with the mind and character of a people. Judging against this clear-cut distinction will not lead us far because dreams could express individual's desires and anxieties but the symbolic mode of expression takes recourse at times to the primordial or archetypal images which mankind has retained over the ages in its subconscious. The subconscious thus is the meeting point of individual's responses to the external stimuli as also his inalienable linkage to the mankind at large. Myths also bank upon some archetypal images and motifs. Important critics of this school include Northrop Frye, Richard Chase, Joseph Campbell, etc.

Archetypal criticism emerged in the 1930s, inspired by the archetypal psychology of the Swiss analytical psychologist C.G. Jung (1875-1961). Its first **application to literature** is to be found in Maud Bodkin's *Archetypal Patterns in Poetry* (1934). The book sought to prioritize archetypal over the mythological. According to the John Hopkins *Guide to Literary Theory and Criticism*, the archetype is the "tendency to form and reform images in relation to certain kinds of repeated experience, which may vary in individual cultures, authors and readers" (65). In the context of literature, these are also the images that commonly occur in other literary works. In his search for universal archetypes in texts, he scanned texts even of the fourth century like Shepherd of Hermas and sometimes grossly generalized them for saking issues of genre, period or language. Jung's own contribution to literary criticism was on German thinker-writer Goethe's Faust which he believed to be an expression of the writer's personal myth. It may be pointed out here that outside the domain of psychology, Jungian theory did not provide any clear-cut ways of psychological analysis of literature. Major archetypal critics include James Hillman, William Bickman, Henri Corbin, Gilbert Durand, etc. Some of the important archetypal studies in literature include Elizabeth Drew's study of T.S. Eliot, June Singer's of William Blake, and Bettina Knapp's criticism of Persian and some European texts in her *Jungian Approach to Literature* (1984). The British journal *Spring: A Journal of Archetype and Culture* is devoted to such studies. In 1980s, feminism also drew inspiration from archetypal criticism, as can be judged from Annis Pratt's *Archetypal Patterns in Women's Fiction* (1981).

Some examples of the **images** probed in archetypal criticism will not be out of place here. The image of water, for instance, occurs most commonly in different myths. It occurs in the form of sea, rivers, springs, etc. Water is the source of life. Myths of creation and destruction are related to sea, the biggest reservoir of water. A river, apart from being a symbol of death and rebirth, also stands for the eternity. According to Jung, water is also the commonest symbol for the unconscious. Similarly, sun stands for creative energy. It also betokens law in nature as it rises and sets and changes direction according to a set pattern. Spiritual and intellectual wisdom is denoted by it. It also represents time and life. While rising sun represents creation and enlightenment, the setting sun represents death. Similarly, while tree stands for regeneration, desert is for aridity and death. Colours have, since time immemorial, represented certain feelings. Thus, white colour stands for purity, innocence and infinity, red colour is for violent passion and sacrifice. Again,while green is for growth, fertility and hope, black is for darkness, evil and death. Images do not have fixed meanings; they have meanings according to the context.

Taking up archetypal **motifs**, one finds these prevalent in all cultures, as for example, the archetype of creation which forms the basis of most of the myths in the world. It refers to how the universe was created and man was made by a supernatural agency. Similarly, the archetypes of heaven and hell are also common to most cultural myths. While the archetype of cyclical time is integral to Hinduism, several myths linked to the repetition of seasons are found in ancient Egyptian and European myths. Such a mythical frame involving birth-death-rebirth was used with regard to Christ. The vegetation myth used by T.S. Eliot is also related to the change of seasons. A common archetype is that of a hero who undertakes a long and arduous journey, fights battles with demons and monsters or solves riddles that defy answer.

Northrop Frye (1912-91), in his *Anatomy of Criticism* (1957), developed a rather complex mix of genres conforming to various season. He drew upon personal and seemingly unrelated archetypal images to develop his concept of 'mythoi', which he explained as the organizing principles of different genres. These genres correspond to various seasons, as for example, comedy is linked to spring season, romance to summer, tragedy to autumn and satire to winter. Thus, Frye identifies myth with literature, asserting that an archetype is basically an element of literary experience. In *The Stubborn Structure* (1970), he claims that "mythology as a whole provides a kind of diagram or blueprint of what literature as a whole is all about, an imaginative survey of the human situation from the beginning to the end, from the height to the depth, of what is imaginatively conceivable" (Guerin et al., 191). Frye continued to work on his archetypal theory, with the intent to apply it to contemporary poets as also to Biblical texts. It must be pointed out here that Frye has tried to distance himself from the archetypal content of Jungian formulations even though he borrowed from him the archetypes of persona, anima, counselor and shadow and called his own theory as Jugnian criticism.

Works Cited

Frye, Northrop. *The Stubborn Critic: Essays on Criticism and Society*, 1970, Oxen: Routledge, 2011.

Guerin, Wilfred L. et al. *A Handbook of Critical Approaches to Literature*, fifth edition. New Delhi: Oxford University Press, 2006.

Reeves, Charles Eric. "Myth Theory and Criticism" *John Hopkins Guide to Literary Theory & Criticism*. Second Edition. Eds. Groden, Michael et al. Baltimore: The John Hopkins University Press, 2005.

Watts, Alan W. *Myth and Ritual in Christianity*. New York: Beacon, 1954.

11
Feminist Criticism

'Feminism' takes a hard look at the real position of women in society which discriminates against women mainly due to sexual difference. The 'women's movement' of the 1960s was not, of course, the start of feminism. It can be seen as a climax of an old tradition of thought and action which finds mention in some books. These books had diagnosed the problems of women's inequality in society and proposed solutions too.

One of the **earliest works** is Mary Wollstonecraft's *A Vindication of the Rights of Woman* (1792). She was prompted to write the book to counter a report presented by Talleyrand-Perigord to the French Assembly which sought only domestic education for women. In her dedication of the book to the writer of the report, she maintained that her arguments were dictated by a disinterested spirit: "I plead for my sex—not for myself...," she writes. This, as also Virginia Woolf's *A Room of One's Own* (1929), vividly portrayed the unequal treatment given to women and rued the neglect of education for women.Woolf maintains in her book that "a woman must have money and room of her own if she is to write fiction" (13). In other words, women will not be able to write well and freely until they have privacy, space and freedom. A more radical critique came from Simone de Beauvoir with her book *The Second Sex* (1949), which pointed out how the woman is treated as the 'Other' in our society while man retains the position of adominating 'subject'.

A number of writings and theories related to feminism have appeared so that instead of the term 'feminism', scholars now prefer 'feminisms'. The leading lights of this movement include writers and critics like Elaine Showalter, Kate Millet, Helene Cixous, Juliet Mitchell, Luce Irigaray, etc. Some of the common **assumptions and concepts** of the movement are given below.

1. The basic view is that the Western society is partriarchal, that is, it is male-centred and controlled by men. It is organized and conducted in such a way that women are subordinated to man in all cultural fields—familial, religious, political, economic, social, legal, artistic, etc.
2. A distinction is drawn between sex and gender. Since the time the Bible was written or Greek philosophical texts were produced, she has been defined as the Other. The feminists believe that while one's sex is determined by anatomy, the traits that are supposed to constitute masculinity or femininity are cultural constructs. As Simone de Beauvior put it, "One is not born, but rather becomes a woman.... It is civilization as a whole that produces this creature.... Which is described as feminine" (295).
3. Toril Moi, the feminist literary critic, draws an important distinction between the terms 'feminist', 'female' and 'feminine'. As she explains, the first is 'a political position', the second 'a matter of biology', and the third 'a set of culturally defined characteristics'. The force of feminism lies particularly in the distinction between the second and the third.
4. Another point is that this patriarchal or androcentric ideology pervades traditional literature, particularly that which has been considered great. Literary works, regarded as the most important ones, focus on male protagonists—Oedipus, Ulysses, Hamlet, Tom Jones and others. Compared to these male characters, the female characters are marginal and subordinate. So a major interest of feminist critics in English-speaking countries has been to reconstitute the ways in which literature is

dealt with to do justice to female points of view, concerns and values.

The **history** of feminist movement can be briefly touched here. Women's movement has generally been divided into three stages. The first wave of women's movement started in the 19th and early 20th century in the U.K. in which women demanded right to vote and own property. The second wave started in the 1960s and 1970s in the U.S.A. which lasted till the 1990s in which women sought to liberate themselves from the traditional roles of wife and mother. In the feminist criticism of the 1970s, the major effort went into exposing what might be called the mechanisms of patriarchy, that is, the mindset in men and women which perpetuated sexual inequality. Critical attention was given to books written by male writers in which stereotypical images of women were constructed. Then, in the 1980s, feminism became an eclecticfield and it drew upon the findings and approaches of other kinds of criticism—Marxism, structuralism, linguistics, and so on. It also shifted its focus from attacking male versions of the world to exploring the nature of the female world and outlook, and reconstructing the lost or suppressed records of female experience. This led to the need to construct anew canon of women's writing by rewriting the history of the novel and of poetry in such a way that neglected writers were given prominence.

Things underwent a sea-change in 1990s, when Rebecca Walker, an African-American activist and daughter of the writer Alice Walker, coined the term 'Third Wave' and also set up the Third Wave Foundation. She stressed the need for incorporating the voices of many young women, non-heterosexual and women of colour. In a nutshell, feminist criticism has grown "to encompass a vast series of concerns: a rewriting of literary history so as to include the contributions of women; the tracing of a female literary tradition; theories of sexuality and sexual difference, drawing on psycho-analysis, Marxism, and the social sciences; the representation of women in male literature; the role of gender in both literary creation and literary criticism...the connection between gender and various aspects of literary form, such as genre and meter..." (Habib: 2008, 43) and so on.

A major division within feminist criticism has concerned disagreements about the amount and type of theory that should feature in it. This has been evident in its variants like **English, American and French Feminisms.** What is usually called the 'Anglo-American' version of feminism has tended to be more skeptical about recent critical theory than that of the 'French' feminism. The French feminists have adopted and adapted a great deal of post-structuralist and psychoanalytic criticism as the basis of much of their work. The Anglo-Americans maintain a major interest in traditional critical concepts like theme, motif and characterization. They see the close reading and explication of individual literary texts as the major business of feminist criticism. However, British feminist criticism is often distinctly different from American feminism, where the feminist criticism was inaugurated by Mary Ellman's witty discussion, in *Thinking about Women* (1968) and it also took the shape of much tangible political action. British feminist criticism tends to be 'socialist feminist', aligned with cultural materialism or Marxism. While the works in the so-called Anglo-American tradition appeared in the late 1970s, the British 'Socialist feminist' tradition produced its key works in the mid-1980s and it still remains active and influential.

In contrast to the Americans, the work of French feminism is more overtly theoretical. It takes as its starting-point the insights of major poststructuralists, especially Lacan, Foucault and Derrida. For these feminist critics, the literary text is never a representative of reality, or an expression of personal experience. Indeed, the French theorists write about language, representation, psychology, etc. before coming to the text itself. In this respect, Elaine Showalter observes, "English feminist criticism, essentially Marxist, stresses opposition; French feminist criticism, essentially psychoanalytic, stresses repression; American feminist criticism, essentially textual, stresses expression" (Guerin et al., 226). The major figures in 'French' feminism are Julia Kristeva, Helene Cixous, and Luce Irigaray.

Another fundamental issue is the question of whether or not there exists a form of **language** which is inherently feminine. Virginia Woolf, for example, says that language use is gendered, so that when a woman turns to novel writing, she finds that there is no "common sentence ready for use" (82). Generally, the female writer is seen as suffering the handicap of having to use a medium which is fashioned for the male. The thesis that language is 'masculine' in this sense was developed by Dale Spender in the early 1980s in her book *Man Made Language* (1981). However, this view is challenged by Sandra Gilbert and Susan Gubar in the essay "Sexual Linguistics: Gender, Language, Sexuality" (1989). But if language is male-oriented, how can we have a female-oriented language is a million-dollar question.

The impact of Marxism on feminism has been a matter of some confusion because of the different areas of relationships with which both are concerned. While Marxism is centred on the relationship between labour and capital, women's relationships centre primarily on the gender. **Michele Barrett**, in her *Marxist Feminist Analysis* (1980) lays stress on three points which are at the root of Marxist feminist approach. These have been mentioned as patriarchy, reproduction and ideology. The economic organization of households and the division of labour in it are seen as directed at the oppression of women. The state machinery and the education system do little to mitigate the predicament of women.

Elaine Showalter (b. 1941), an American literary critic, in her book *Towards a Feminist Poetics* (1979) describes the change in the late 1970s as a shift from 'andro-texts' (books by men) to 'gyno-texts' (books by women). She coined the term 'gynocritics', which meant the study of writing by women. The scope of gynocriticism includes "the history, styles, themes, genres, and structures of writing by women; the psychodynamics of female creativity; the evolution or laws of a female literary tradition" (311). Showalter also identifies three phases in women's writing. The first is a *feminine phase* (1840-80), in which women writers imitated dominant male artistic norms and aesthetic standards. The second was a *feminist phase* (1880-1920), in which radical and often distinct positions were maintained. The third was a *female phase* (1920 onwards) which looked particularly at female writing and female experience. Showalter also describes four current models of difference taken up by many feminists around the world: biological, linguistic, psychoanalytic, and cultural.

It will be seen that the French theorists have particularly assumed the existence of an *ecriture feminine*. The term, according to Showalter, literally means women's writing, more precisely, the inscription of the female body and female difference in language and text. Another French feminist **Helene Cixous** (b. 1937) first coined this term in her essay "The Laugh of the Medusa" (1975), where she asserts "woman must write herself, must write about women, and bring women to writing from which they have been driven away as violently as their bodies" (2039), because their sexual pleasure has been repressed and denied expression. This kind of writing is somehow uniquely the product of female physiology, which women must celebrate in their writing. **Julia Kristeva** (b. 1941) focusses more on the linguistic aspect and uses the terms *symbolic* and *semiotic* for the two aspects of language. The symbolic aspect is associated with authority, order, father, repression and control. By contrast, the semiotic aspect of discourse is characterized not by logic and order but a loose way of writing, one which increases the available range of possibilities. For the terms 'semiotic' and 'symbolic', Kristeva is indebted to Lacan and his distinction between the 'imaginary' and the 'symbolic'.

The relationship between feminism and psychology was brought to the fore by **Kate Millet's** (b. 1934) *Sexual Politics* (1969), in which she condemned Freud as the prime source of patriarchal attitudes against women. However, **Juliet Mitchell** (b. 1940) defends Freud in her book *Psychoanalysis and Feminism* (1974). Millet argues that the notion of penis-envy need not be taken as simply the male physical organ itself. Rather it should be considered as an emblem of social power and the advantages that go with it. **Sandra Gilbert** (b. 1936) and **Susan Gubar** (b. 1944) use the idea of 'social castration' which means the same thing, i.e. women's lack of social power. Postcolonial approach is seen in the women's texts, particularly in *Other Worlds* (1987) by **Gayatri Spivak** (b. 1944). Jane Gallop's (b. 1952) book *Feminism and Psychoanalysis* (1982) adopts Lacanian variety of psychoanalysis, i.e. the phallus is not considered a physical biological object but a symbol of power. In general, the defence of Freud and Lacan has been more favourably received by the French and British feminists than by the Americans.

Feminist theoretical and critical writings are recent in origin but newer versions of these keep appearing off and on in the world. There exist a number of specialized feminist journals and publishing houses. Almost all colleges and universities now have programmes in women's studies and courses in women's literature and feminist criticism. An increasingly important place is assigned to writings by and about women in anthologies, periodicals and conferences. The concern with "the effects of sexual differences, in writing, interpretation, analysis, and assessment of literature," observes M.H. Abrams, "seems destined to have the most prominent and enduring effects on literary history criticism, and academic instruction, when conducted by men as well as by women" (105).

Works Cited

Abrams, M.H. and Geoffrey Galt Harpham. *A Handbook of Literary Terms*. New Delhi: Cengage Learning, 2009.

Beauvoir, Simon de. *The Second Sex*, Second Edition. London: Vintage, 1997.

Cixous, Helene. "The Laugh of the Medusa" *Norton Anthology of Theory & Criticism*. New York: W.W. Norton, 2001.

Guerin, Wilfred L. et al. *A Handbook of Critical Approaches to Literature*, Fifth edition. New Delhi: Oxford University Press, 2006.

Habib, M.A.R. *Modern Literary Criticism and Theory: A History*. New Delhi: Wiley India, 2008, Reprint, 2013.

Showalter, Elaine. "Feminist Criticism in the Wilderness". *Modern Criticism & Theory: A Reader*. Second Edition. Eds. David Lodge & Nigel Wood. Delhi: Pearson Education, 1988, pp. 308-30.

Wollstonecraft, Mary. *A Vindication of the Rights of Women*. London: W.W. Norton & Co., 1792, Reprint, 1988.

Woolf, Virginia. *A Room of One's Own*. New Delhi: Foundation, 2001.

12

Feminism in India

Feminism in India is an issue on which varied opinions have been expressed. As a mode of activism and at one end of the spectrum, it is believed to be the fallout of the movement in the West, confined to the elite class, with nothing indigenous about it, while on the other, references to pre-history and historical times are sought to buttress the view that women have had an equal status with men. But Indian Feminism, as a theoretical genre, has few takers and there is dearth of theoretical analyses which can be called uniquely Indian.

Taking up feminist activism on the ground level, which gives strength to theoretical study, it is not difficult to perceive movements aimed at defending equal opportunities to women in political, economic, and social fields. Like their feminist counterparts all over the world, feminists in India also seek the right to work for equal wages, the right to equal access to health and education, and equal political rights. They have fought against the discriminatory laws like the law of inheritance.

Indian culture contains **mythical and scriptural references** to the exalted position of women like goddesses Laxmi, Durga and Saraswati. Ancient philosophical treatises refer to Gargi, Maitrayee, etc., who were great scholars. It is interesting to note that the women associated with the *bhakti* movement defied all restrictions and even challenged caste and patriarchy. Meera, Avvaiyar and Karaikal Ammaiyar, for instance, protested against patriarchy and subverted the hegemonic structures by staying outside the domain of marriage. There are also historical instances of powerful women like the queen of Jhansi, fondly called Jhansi ki Rani, who fought the British valiantly, to the modern-day Prime Minister Indira Gandhi, one of the few women heads of governments in the world in her time. Thus, the concept of women being powerful is not new to Indian society, and yet due to the dichotomy between practice and protestation, the position of women at large in society has not improved significantly.

The **history of feminism** in India is normally divided into three phases: the first phase, began with the establishment of Bramho Sabha in 1828, the precursor to Bramho Samaj, by reformists like Raja Ram Mohan Roy and others. Roy thought that superstitions and obnoxious practices like the *Sati*, child marriage and casteism brought a bad name to Hindu religion. He also demanded equal inheritance laws for women. But there was also opposition to Western education and Western concepts also as these emanated from the colonizers. Social and spiritual reformers like Jyotiba Phule (1827-90), Swami Dayanand Saraswati (1824-83) and Swami Vivekananda (1863-1902) tried to change the general mindset towards women and laid stress on women's education. Thus, men initiated social reform movements against various social evils.

The second phase began in 1915 when Mahatma Gandhi involved women in the Quit India Movement. This was the period of intense politicization of masses. During this period, the struggle against colonial rule intensified. Nationalism became the pre-eminent cause. Claiming Indian superiority to inspire resistance to the colonial rulers also meant going back to the conservative models of womanhood. Gandhi legitimised and expanded women's public activities by initiating them into the non-violent civil disobedience movement. At the same time, he also exalted their feminine roles of caring, self-abnegation, sacrifice and tolerance; and carved a niche for those in the public arena. Women-only organisations like All India Women's Conference (AIWC) and the National Federation of Indian Women (NFIW) emerged. Women engaged themselves with issues relating to the scope of women's political participation, women's franchise, etc. It would be right to say of this phase that "In India, feminism and nationalism were closely inter-linked.... The women's movement in India had none of the man-woman antagonism characteristic of woman's movement in the West" (Chaudhuri, xxi).

The second decade of the twentieth century was a new era for Indian women and is defined as 'feminism' that was responsible for the creation of localised women's associations. These associations emphasised women's education issues, developed livelihood strategies for working-class women, and also organised national level women's associations such as the AIWC. AIWC was closely affiliated with the Indian National Congress. Under the leadership of Mahatma Gandhi, it worked within the nationalist and anti-colonialist freedom movements. This made the mass mobilisation of women an integral part of Indian nationalism.

The third and final phase starts after the attainment of independence, when several women's organizations took up the cause of women's uplift. The record of the political parties in this respect has been uneven and has been mostly driven by the desire to get votes from traditionally patriarchal social set-up. To a large extent, the emerging feminist movement in India was influenced by **Western ideals**. These called for education and equal rights, but also adapted their appeals to local issues and concerns such as dowry-related violence against women, *Sati*, sex selective abortion and custodial rape. Feminist class-consciousness also came into focus, with feminists recognising the inequalities not just between men and women but also within power structures such as caste, tribe, language, religion, region, class, etc. Despite the progress made on this front, women living in India today face discrimination in practically every field—legal, educational, social and cultural.

Post-independence, the constitution-makers of India saw to it that women got equal rights as citizens of India. They also had voting rights and did not have to struggle for basic rights as did women in the West. The political parties, in order to expand their base, created **women's wings** in the name of promoting women's welfare. The All India Women's Conference continued to operate and in 1954 the Indian Communist Party formed its own women's wing known as the National Federation of Indian Women. In 1975, All India Progressive Women's Association was formed by the radical Communist Party (Marxist Leninist). However, feminist agendas and movements became less active right after India's 1947 independence, as the nationalist agendas of nation building took precedence over feminist issues. Prior to independence, most feminists accepted the sexual divide within the labour force. However, feminists in the 1970s challenged the inequalities. These inequalities included unequal wages for women and relegation of women to 'unskilled' spheres of work.

Despite these signs of progress on the feminist front, **problems** still continue to obstruct women from fully taking advantage of new rights and opportunities in India. There are many traditions and customs that often conflict with the constitutional guarantees and legal benefits. Traditionally, women have been taught to emulate the Sita-Savitri model of ancient times without expecting anything from husbands. Indian society is largely composed of hierarchical systems within families and society. These are based upon age, sex, relationships within families, and at the societal level, on caste, lineage, wealth, occupation, and political clout. Evil practices like dowry, child marriage, etc. still continue in society. Despite legal framework to provide reservation to women in local bodies like Panchayats and municipal corporations, the real work is often taken over by their husbands. The bill for reservation of women in the legislatures and the Parliament is still held up.

Women, mostly from middle class, have entered and indeed discharged themselves brilliantly in every field, be it education, medicine, engineering, defence, art, literature or any other area. Despite their economic empowerment, they have not got the recognition at the level of family. However, the uneducated and rural section of the Indian society, which forms a major percentage of the total population, women are seen as an economic burden. Their contributions to productivity are mostly invisible as their familial and domestic contributions are unfairly overlooked. Due to high illiteracy rate among women, they get lower wages and mostly work as unskilled or semi-skilled labourers. Moreover, the caste-based politics of the country has created a yawning gulf between different castes. Dalit groups allege discrimination and hold higher classes responsible for their backwardness. Women within Dalit castes have formed organizations such as the All India Dalit Women's Forum and the National Federation of Dalit Women and Dalit Solidarity, which focus on the gendered implications of caste-based violence and oppression.

The **difference** between Indian feminism and the Western feminism hinges basically on the fact that the individual in the West is an independent entity, whereas in India, an individual is usually considered to be just part of the family and kinship pattern and even the survival of the individual is dependent upon cooperation. Women's movements in India have often juxtaposed Indian feminism with Western feminism. A number of scholars have focused on the Indian sensitivity as the distinguishing mark of Indian feminism. It is this feature of Indian womanhood which is responsible for a woman placing the interests of the family above her own to the extent of self-negation. The polar opposites of man/woman stands disputed in the Indian context. If it was men who initiated social reform movements against various social evils, it is the women in the family who perpetrate violence against women in the form of infamous 'bride burning' episodes to avenge low dowry, or go in for abortion to avoid giving birth to female babies. It should however be noted that several communities in India such as the Nairs of Kerala, Shettys of Mangalore, certain Maratha clans and tribes of North-eastern India exhibit matriarchal tendencies. In these communities, the head of the family is the oldest woman rather than the oldest man.

In **modern Indian literature**, one finds portrayal of women according to the ethos of the time. Rabindranath Tagore's (1861-1941) women, though they suffer due to traditional stranglehold, are often in love with freedom and are outspoken too, as for example, in the play *Chandalika*. Aurobindo (1872-1950) raised the spirit of rebellion in women to the celestial level in his epic poem *Savitri*. The spirit of freedom struggle percolated into Raja Rao's (1908-2006) *Kanthapura*, which shows women characters motivated by the Gandhian call for Satyagraha.

Post-independence writers like Rath Prawer Jhabvala (1927-2013), Kamala Markandaya (1924-2004), Anita Desai's (b. 1937), Shashi Deshpande (b. 1938) have been concerned about the plight of women of different sections of society. Mostly, women characters are shown suffering in mute silence but in a few cases they speak up. Poets like Kamala Das have boldly spoken of women's body. Contemporary writers like Arundhati Roy, and Manju Kapur have shown relationships like cross-community and same-sex ones which are not accepted in society.Bharati Mukherjee, Chitra Banerjeee Divakaruni, Jhumpa Lahiri, etc. talk about the Diasporic women. It will be seen that it is mostly the women writers who have dealt with feminist themes.

The indigenous literature produced in **regional languages** is quite rich in feminist content and there are male writers also here, as for example, the Bengali novelist Sharat Chandra Chatterjee, who was even referred to as a woman in man's body. Amrita Pritam from Punjab was known for her bold lifestyle and expression. Poet Maithili Sharan Gupt valorized Urmila, Laxman's wife, who was left behind while Sita left for the forest with her husband Rama. He also focused on Yashoda (Gautam Buddha's wife) in this way and even presented Kaikeyi in a new light. Jai Shankar Prasad is another poet who made Kamayani and not Manu the protagonist of his eponymous long poem. There are poets and writers like Jainendra, Mridula Garg, Chitra Mudgil, Nasira Sharma, etc. who have taken up the cause of women in Hindi literature.

Despite these impressive articulations of women's point of view, the Indian **theoretical landscape** looks rather barren. For one, in keeping with the complexities of Indian situation, it would be right to speak of feminisms' rather than 'feminism' here also, as in the wide world. No doubt, the emergence of Third World feminism joined the existing feminist movements with the rest of the world besides giving birth to newer ideas. Various Indian writers have attempted to define feminism from the Indian standpoint. According to Kamla Bhasin and Nighat Said Khan, it is "an awareness of women's oppression and exploitation in society, at work and within the family, and conscious action by women and men to change this situation" (Chaudhuri, 4). Chandra Talpade Mohanty, an Indian academic teaching in the US, defines feminism in terms of relationships: "The relationship between 'Woman'—a cultural and ideological composite Other, constructed through diverse representational discourses (scientific, literary, juridical, linguistic, cinematic, etc.)—and 'women'—real, material subjects of their collective histories—is one of the central questions the practice of feminist scholarship seeks to address" (Ghosh).

Gayatri Chakravorty Spivak (b. 1942), an Indian professor teaching in the USA, has been one of the leading poststructuralist writers. Her work with poststructuralism, Marxism and feminism has resulted in what Pramod Nayar calls "cult texts in the postcolonial canon" (171). Her book *In Other Worlds* (1987) and essays like "Three Women's Texts", "Feminism and Deconstruction", "Subaltern Studies: Deconsructing Historiogrphay", etc. reveal her feminist views. Her essay "Can the Subaltern Speak?" underlines the incapability of the colonized to speak up. This theoretical formulation is also applied to the condition of women in liberated Third World countries including India, where structures of power inhibit the subaltern to articulate his predicament. Women are doubly challenged on account of their so-called 'weaker sex'. The prevailing patriarchal discourse comes in the way of her true representation. If she has to speak up, she must do so inside the domineering discourse which is not of her making and is out of her control. She, therefore, is for a different approach towards the subaltern/women.

Spivak uses Gramsci's term 'subaltern' for anyone who has no status outside the discourse. The position of the subaltern is represented by the elite intellectual, which is a kind of 'epistemic violence'. Spivak would rather have women subsist on the margins than being represented by others, because that would keep her for ever on the margins. The reason for this reticence is that Spivak, as a poststructuralist, knows the opaque nature of writing, which does not permit clear and innocent communication. A writing gets interpreted within the discourse controlled by structures of power. The way s/he is being talked about in the Western discourse, it is clear that a romantic construct of the subaltern is being created which is far from real. When the British colonizers talked about the practice of 'sati' in India, they wanted to appear as saviours for the native woman, and thereby legitimize their imperialism. Later, when the nationalists used the voice of the women for their own purpose; she was still left in the lurch.

While deconstructing Mahashweta Devi's story "Draupadi" in her book *In Other Worlds*, Spivak observes in her characteristic opaque style that if the peasant insurgent was the victim and also the hero of anti-imperialism in India, then "for reasons of collusion between pre-existing structures of patriarchy and transnational capitalism, it is the urban sub-proletarian female who is the paradigmatic subject of the current configuration of the International Division of Labour" (300). Thus, she re-defines the subjectivity of the subaltern female. On the other hand, while analyzing Devi's other story "Breast-Giver", Spivak shows the limits of what she calls elite "Western Marxist-Feminism, Western Liberal Feminism, and French high theory of the Female Body" (333). Applying elite methodologies to 'subaltern material', according to her, might lead to "continued subalternization of so-called 'third world' literatures" (333). Thus, she finds the contemporary theories lacking in understanding the Indian reality and underlines the cultural difference, hinting obliquely at the need for an ethical approach to the issue.

Jasbir Jain, a well-known academic, has traced the history of feminism in India in her book *Indigenous Roots of Feminism: Culture, Subjectivity and Agency* (2011). She believes that Indian women are defined by "a variety of roles and classifications —caste, class, urban, rural, tribal, education and its absence, married, abandoned, widowed or divorced, single, dependent or economically independent, barren or productive, lesbian or heterosexual—the list could go on" (2011: 269). She does not like the category of religion because of its divisive tendency, but she finds a long tradition of resistance in religious and secular discourses, personal lives at various levels. Also she is aware of and a participant in contemporary resistance narratives.

Jain is of the opinion that feminist discourse in India has been shaped, on the one hand, by our colonial past, and on the other, by our opposition to foreign domination. Woman's struggle "accounts for the difference from Western feminism and the break from male representations of feminity; they work in cultural contexts and against cultural impositions which deny them space and freedom, self and agency" (2011: 189). Jain is sore over the fact that women have not been 'visible' in our history, as for example, their role has been ignored in the Dalit history and in the Ambedkar movement. "Dalit aesthetics, despite a fair amount of theorisation by the dalits themselves, is falling into a rut even though their writing is ripe of more theorisation" (2002: 224). This has been explained as the dominance of details of protests rather than evolution of any Dalit theory of literature.

Chandra Talpade Mohanty, a feminist academic teaching in the USA, in her essay "Under Western Eyes: Feminist Scholarship and Colonial Discourses" (1986) criticizes the hegemonic feminist discourse of the West. In her essay, Mohanty analyzes the portrayal of the Third World women as presented in Western feminist works. She detects the so-called 'colonialist move' in a number of Western radical and liberal feminist writings, and identifies the premises in those texts which led to the production of the Third World woman as a singular and monolithic subject. Mohanty concludes that the most valuable kind of feminist research ought to avoid specious generalizations about the Third World women or the women in Africa. It should, instead, take into account the lived experiences of specific women as a basis for understanding and theorizing. Experience helps people gain a cultural insight through which they are able to perceive and understand the situation in a better way, rather than relying on a false sense of 'sisterhood of shared experiences'.

Another feminist **Urvashi Butalia** is the co-founder of Kali for Women, which is India's first women's publishing house that publishes Third World studies on women. In her book *The*

Other Side of Silence: Voices from the Partition of India, she has collected interviews of the survivors of the traumatic partition of India which she compares to the European Holocaust. Lakhs of women were raped, tortured and murdered. She finds that rape was taken as a form of 'reprisal' on the minority community. Thus, even though politics was responsible for the division of the country, women fell into the crossfire for no fault of theirs. This continues to be the bane of Indian society even more than six decades after independence. **Ritu Menon**, Butalia's associate in the publishing venture, also wrote *No Woman's Land* (2004), which contains interviews with the women victims from the Indian subcontinent, who suffered due to the partition of India. Besides studies of Muslim women in India, she has also authored *From Mathura to Manorama: Resisting Violence Against Women in India* (2007).

Among other Indian feminist critics, Suma Chitnis in *Feminism in India*, a compilation of essays on the concept of feminism in India, describes how she feels disturbed at the complacent attitude of Indian women and their general "disapproval of feminist anger" (Chaudhuri, 8). **Radha Kumar**, in *History of Doing* (1993) has written on the history of women's movements in India both before and after independence. **Vandana Shiva,** an environmentalist and eco-feminist, in her first book *Staying Alive* (1988) sought to redefine perceptions of women in the Third World. A report "Most Farmers in India are Women" which she wrote for the FAO in 1990 brought to light the well-known, though seldom realized fact of peasantry in India.

As is seen from this brief study that most of the writing is based on empirical study but it lacks theorization. Besides, all the writers and activists in contemporary India happen to be women. It is surprising that while the movement for the uplift of women was started by men, they seem to have withdrawn in the belief that governmental action is adequate for the purpose. Or it is believed that the women have come of age and they can very well articulate their standpoint. Both these suppositions are reasons for disquiet because of the unenviable position of women in Indian society. In today's commerce-driven world, the MNC's are seen to project a homogenous image of ideal women.

This is also manifested in the form of nationalist pride exhibited through Indian women winning international beauty pageants. According to some feminists, such developments have offered women greater sexual autonomy, but many others feel that such commodification of female bodies has only served the purpose of feeding to male fantasies.

Feminism being a Western notion is generally not approved by the people here, but it is also a fact that no one questions the imported concepts of "the parliamentary or presidential systems; of the development of capitalism; of private ownership of land and absentee landlordism; or of the ideology of the Left. The western origins of Einstein, or Marx or Lenin have never made their ideas irrelevant for us. Nor should they be considered irrelevant or out of context, for an idea cannot be confined within national or geographic boundaries" (Ghosh).

It would be right to conclude that feminism around the world has been portioned out by intellectuals, but in India it is the political affiliations which have divided women's movements even as these have grown in number. This fact as also the strong traditional forms of family and social structures have made the task of resisting male hegemony and providing true succor to women very difficult. Moreover, the absence of any committed feminists and the scarcity of feminists theory texts too is responsible for the weak manifestation of feminism in India.

Works Cited

Chaudhuri, Maitrayee, ed. *Feminism in India*. 2004. New Delhi: Kali for Women & Women Unlimited, 2006.

Nayar, Pramod. *Contemporary Literary and Cultural Theory: From Structuralism to Ecocriticism*. New Delhi: Longman, 2011.

Mohanty, Chandra Talpade. "Under Western Eyes: Feminist Scholarship and Colonial Discourses." *Feminist Review*, No. 30 (1988): 61-88. JSTOR 10 July 2013. <http://www.jstor.org/stable/1395054>

Jain, Jasbir. *Writing Women Across Cultures*. Jaipur and New Delhi: Rawat Publications, 2002.

———. *Indigenous Roots of Feminism: Culture, Subjectivity and Agency*. New Delhi: Sage, 2011.

Ghosh, Arpita. "Indian Feminism: A Debate on the Incorporation of the 'alien' Culture within the 'native' Tradition". Muse India, Issue 50: July-Aug. 2013 accessed 11 July 2013. <http://museindia.com/regularcontent.asp?issid=34&id=2311>

Spivak, Gayatri Chakravorty. *In Other Worlds*. New York: Routledge, 1998, Reprint, 2012.

13

Gender Studies/ Queer Theory

The term 'Gender Studies' is an umbrella term for all the theories dealing with genders—male, female, neutar, as also fringe groups commonly referred to as queer. The basic premise of this area of studies is that while sex is determined by nature, gender is constructed by society and should not involve any discrimination. Gender criticism, part of gender studies, analyzes "differing conceptions of gender and their role in the writing, reception, subject matter, and evaluation of literary works" (Abrams, 119).

The **lesbian and gay theories** began with a social movement. The Stonewall Riots of 1969 may be described as the point of origin of the gay liberation movement. The riots broke out when police raided the Stonewall Tavern in New York City. Many gays, lesbians and transvestites fought back. Since 1970s, the gay liberation movement has sought to fight social, legal, medical and religious oppression and tried to locate a whole new cultural space for the so far marginalized community. The journal *College English* brought out a special issue on gay writing and politics in 1974. The publication of Foucault's *The History of Sexuality* (1978) and the rise of feminist theory were also significant moments in the development of gay/lesbian theory.

Going back into history, one finds a number of **ancient writers** in whose works the homosexual tendencies are manifest. Even in the ancient Greece, Plato and Sappho are marked for this inclination. In European literature, Andre Gide, Marcel Proust, Walt Whitman, W.H. Auden, Virginia Woolf, etc. fall in this category. William Shakespeare's references to the Earl of Southampton are well known as camouflaging homosexual intentions. Indeed, one of the pet projects of the gay/lesbian movements has been to question the essentialist assumption that heterosexuality is the only universal norm and homosexuality is a later-day deviation.

The group called **Radicalesbians** stressed the need for a field of study that would be different from feminism because as they saw it, feminism had sidelined lesbianism. To them, lesbianism was the real answer to the problems highlighted by feminism, that is, women condemning men for their patriarchal views could, after all, stay with women. In an essay "Compulsory Heterosexuality and Lesbian Existence" (1980), the lesbian feminist poet and theorist Adrienne Rich introduced the idea that "sexuality is a continuum—not a fixed and static set of binary oppositions" (Abrams, 254) to denote a range of experiences between women. Women could lend practical and political support to one another, bond against male tyranny, and share a rich inner life. In *This Sex Which is Not One* (1977), Lucy Irigaray also urged the autonomous existence of lesbians.

The decade of 1980s also saw the establishment of **gender studies**, which had roots in feminist theory. It was based upon Simon de Beauvoir's view that one is not born a woman but becomes one and that gender is a social construct. This view had so far been applied to the area of feminist studies, but it was now interpreted to mean that there could be a woman in man's body and the sexual preferences could be different. Lesbian critics like Bonnie Zimmerman criticized the notion that some essential female identity traits formed the basis of differences of race, class and sexuality. Inspired by the pre-existing field of women's studies, a corresponding area for the male, called Men's Studies was also formed in this decade. There were periods of conflict between the two gender-based groups but finally, the scope of women's studies was broadened to gender studies.

According to feminists and gender critics, **nature vs. culture** binary is implicit in the relationship. Society portrays binary oppositions like masculine and feminine or straight and gay as natural categories, but as David Richter notes, "the rules have little to do with nature and everything to do with culture" (qtd. Guerin et al., 237). The word *homosexual* has only a short history of one hundred years or so, and *heterosexual* is even newer. In any given culture, many critics point out that what is 'normal' sexually depends upon when and where one lives. For example, sodomy was practised by the nobles of Periclean Athens, who had also sexual relationships with women and both sorts of relations were socially accepted. Ross C. Murfin is also of the view that gender is a construct, "an effect of language, a culture, and its institutions" (*ibid.*).

Lesbianism has been a stumbling block for other feminists, and lesbian feminists have at times excluded heterosexual feminists. Some lesbians define lesbianism as the 'normal' relation of woman to woman. They see heterosexuality as 'abnormal'. This has led some heterosexual feminists to reject lesbian perspectives. But, on the whole, lesbian critics have guided other feminists into new appreciation of certain female traits in writing. They have also brought to the forefront the works of the lesbian authors.

Lesbian critics reject the notion of the unified whole. The investigation of text is for locating such **textual features** as mirror images, secret codes, dreams, and narratives of identity. They are drawn to neologisms, unconventional grammar, and other experimental techniques. The practice is also referred to as queer reading. Like other feminists, they stress ambiguity and open-endedness of narratives and seek double meanings. Lesbian critics suggest new genres for study such as the female Gothic or female Utopia. They are often drawn to such experimental women writers as Woolf, Stein, Radclyffe

Hall, and Dajuna Barnes, and to such popular genres as science fiction.

The term **Queer Theory** is an inclusive term for the gay and lesbian studies "together with the theoretical and critical writings about all modes of variance—such as cross-dressing, bisexuality, and trans-sexuality from society's normative model of sexual identity, orientation and activities" (Abrams, 253). To begin with the gays, i.e. homosexual men differentiated themselves from the lesbians, i.e. homosexual women. The latter even despised the former taking them as part of the patriarchal culture, but the societal prejudice towards both brought them together.

In the late 1980s, when the AIDS epidemic broke out in the world, the Simon Watney, Donna Haraway and others attempted to analyze its presentation in the media. It provided the gays and lesbians with a common term around which to unite. They chose the title queer and transformed it into a slogan with pride. It was "a derisive term subversively adopted as a positive designation" (Habib, 139). The term 'queer' was used in a derogatory sense because sexual act between persons belonging to the same sex did not carry approval in the West also, but with the passage of time, the situation has changed and sexual choice is supposed to be a private and personal affair.

Following Foucault, **Queer theorists** view sexuality as disengaged from gender altogether and from the binary opposition of male/female. Judith Butler's *Gender Trouble* (1990) regards all genders as cultural performances. For Butler, gender is "not something one is, it is something one does, or more exactly, a sequence of acts, a verb rather than a noun, a 'doing' rather than a 'being'" (25). A more radical kind of approach in the form of queer theory emerged in the 1990s, with a conference on this subject at the University of California. It more clearly emphasized sexuality rather than gender in the formation of identity. Writers like Lee Edelman deconstructed the gay identity in *Homographesis* (1994), while Sedgwick in her *Epistemology of the Closet* (1990) showed the working of homophobia in normal gender system.

The term **'Queer Public'** refers to the self-identified gays, lesbians, bisexuals, transvestites and the transgendered. At the same time, this public has different understanding of the membership at different times. With a commitment only to pleasure, 'queer' rejects the conventions of Western sexual mores. This rejection resembles the late nineteenth century theory of 'art for art's sake'. In recent times, there has also been an attempt to incorporate into the gay/lesbian canon a number of racial and cultural variations—Jewish, Black, Mexican American, Asian immigrants in the West—in the literary manifestation of homosexuality. Thus, non-white writers like Gloria Anzaldua, Audre Lorde, Firdous Kanga, Hanif Quershi find places among white writers. A similar work to anthologise gay/lesbian writing is taking place in other countries. The seminal volume, *Yaraana: Gay Writing from India* (1999) edited by Hoshang Merchant is an important work in this category.

Lesbian/gay criticism tries to analyse texts not only written by lesbian/gay writers but also by **mainstream writers**. These are the texts that portray directly or indirectly lesbian/gay relationship. Psycho-analytic studies of real or fancied homo-erotic tendencies are undertaken using war-time stories and poems that contain homo-erotic elements. Lesbian/gay critics try to expose the hypocritical nature of our society and how these practices are present, though these remain suppressed due to lack of legitimacy in society.

The contribution of queer theory to literary and cultural studies lies in its emphasis on sexuality as a fourth category of analysis—next to race, gender and class. In its emphasis on sexuality, queer theory gives a much sharper edge to an earlier lesbian and gay interest in sexuality. Gay/lesbian studies or the queer theory has occupied an important place in literary theory. A number of journals are now devoted to queer theory and to gay studies and criticism. The field has also become the subject of learned conferences. It has been established in the curriculum of the humanities and social sciences in many colleges and universities.

Works Cited

Abrams, M.H. and Geoffrey Galt Harpham. *A Handbook of Literary Terms*. New Delhi: Cengage Learning, 2009.

Butler, Judith. *Gender Trouble: Feminism and the Subversion of Identity*. New York: Routledge, 1990.

Habib, M.A.R. *Modern Literary Criticism and Theory: A History*. Oxford: Blackwell, 2008, Reprint, 2013.

Guerin, Wilfred L. et al. *A Handbook of Critical Approaches to Literature*, fifth edition. New Delhi: Oxford University Press, 2006.

14

Phenomenological Criticism

The foundation of phenomenology was laid by the German philosopher Edmund Husserl (1859-1938). The Greek root of the term 'phenomenon' is *phainomenon* which means 'appearance'. Object is nothing in itself; it is only its appearance to us that matters. Hence, phenomenology lays emphasis on examining the ways in which objects appear to the human subject. There is a subjective contribution to this process of appearing. Husserl argues that we cannot be sure of the independent existence of things, but we can be certain of how they appear to our consciousness. Objects can be regarded as things posited, or intended, by our consciousness. All consciousness is consciousness of something. In thinking, one is aware that one's thought is 'pointing towards' some object. The act of thinking and the object of thought are internally related and are mutually dependent and the objects exist only as co-relations of consciousness. To establish certainty about theme, we must first ignore, or 'put in brackets', anything which is not our immediate experience. This is called reduction in the philosophical sense. The question naturally arises as to what is the nature and composition of that which remains behind. To this, Husserl's answer, in his 1917 lecture, is that it is "pure reflection."

We may note that Husserl's **'intentional' theory** of consciousness suggests that 'being' and 'meaning' are always bound up with one another. The world is (being) what I posit or intend (mean). It is to be grasped in relation to me. The world can be viewed from different angles and standpoints. One could see an object from close quarters or a distance, from its side or front, from above or below, past or present. Thus, we can have multiple views of the same object. In his lecture 'Pure Phenomenology, its Method and its Field of Investigation', delivered in 1917, Husserl comments that

> The manner in which the object is given within each of the single intuitions belonging to this continuous consciousness may vary constantly: for example, the object's sensuous 'looks'—the way in which the object always 'looks' different at each approach or remove and at every turning, from above or below, from left or right—may be forever new in the transition from one perception to continuously new perceptions. In spite of that, we have in the way in which such series of perceptions with their changing sensuous images take their courses, intuitive consciousness not of a changing multiplicity but rather of one and the same object that is variously presented.

To put it differently, within the pure immanence of such consciousness, one unitary 'phenomenon' permeates all the manifolds of phenomenal presentation. It is these continuously changing perspectival looks of a real object, which are called phenomena.

According to Terry Eagleton, "Phenomenology…restored the transcendental subject to its rightful throne. The subject was to be seen as the source and origin of all meaning: it was not really itself part of the world, since it brought that world to be in the first place. In this sense, phenomenology recovered and refurbished the old dream of classical bourgeois ideology" (50). Phenomenological criticism is an attempt to apply the phenomenological method to literary works. It aims at wholly **'immanent' reading** of a text, unaffected by anything outside it. All pre-suppositions, whether gained from learning or from common knowledge, must be kept aside to appropriate any immediate experience. "The point here is that it is consciousness that determines objectivity, that classifies and arranges the world of objects and phenomena: wihout this activity, there simply would be no objects as such," comments a critic (Habib, 57). The text is, as such, reduced to a pure embodiment of the author's consciousness. All of its stylistic and semantic aspects are grasped as organic parts of a complex totality, the unifying essence being the author's mind. Phenomenological critics likes Georges Poulet and Jean Starbinski take literature as embodiment of the consciousness of author. Therefore, phenomenological criticism tries to penetrate to the very interior of the writer's consciousness so as to achieve complete objectivity and disinterestedness.

In critical theory, the term phenomenological criticism, also called 'consciousness criticism', is applied specifically to the theory and practice of the **Geneva School** of Critics, most of whose members taught at the University of Geneva. J. Hillis Miller, a colleague of Georges Poulet at John Hopkins University and the leading American representative of the Geneva School of Criticism, applied this critical mode to the analysis of a variety of American and English authors. The Geneva critics regard each work of literature as created out of the *lebenswelt* or the lived experience of its author. It is supposed to embody the author's unique mode of consciousness. In its approach to literature, phenomenology is primarily subjective, and so the phenomenological criticism is opposed to the objective approach of formalism, both in its European form and American new criticism version. Its roots instead go back through the nineteenth century to that type of romantic criticism which regarded a literary work as the revelation of the personality of its author. It also proposed that the awareness of this personality is the chief aim and value of reading literature. Phenomenological approach has been applied to literature by some critics, as for example, J. Hillis Miller in his *Charles Dickens: The World of His Novels* (1959), David Halliburton in *Edgar Allan Poe: A Phenomenological View*, Paul Brodkorb in Ishamael's *White World: A Phenomenological Reading of Moby Dick* (1965), etc.

In the view of the Geneva critics, the distinctive formations of consciousness pervade a work of literature. They manifest themselves in the form of the objects, characters, imagery and style into which the author's personal mode of awareness and feeling imaginatively projects itself. By suspending all pre-existing beliefs and attitudes, the readers of a literary work make themselves purely and passively receptive, and so are capable of achieving participation or even identity with the immanent consciousness of its author. The aim of the Geneva School of critics in a critical reading of the works of literature is described as "consciousness of the consciousness of another". As **Georges Poulet** (1902-91), an important member of the Geneva School puts it, "When I read as I ought.... With the total commitment required of any reader", then "I am thinking the thoughts of another.... My consciousness behaves as though it were the consciousness of another" (qtd. Abrams, 225). Poulet has also tried to trace the history of different treatments of the topic of time in Western literature and his finding is that in each epoch is reflected a consciousness common to all contemporary minds. Also he adds that within this common consciousness, each author attains his/her unique consciousness. In fact, Husserl's attempt was also aimed at identifying the essential features of human consciousness which were shared by all.

Roman Ingarden (1893-1970), a Polish theorist, applied phenomological approach to understand the affective aspect of literature. He believed that a literary text originates from the consciousness in its act of 'intention', which means the consciousness is inclined towards an object. This enables the reader to have the same experience at his end. Not alls text may lead to such an impact because there may be areas with lack of clarity. The reader becomes the creator and fills up such spots in a text.

There is some **difference** in the approach of Husserl and that of the Geneva critics. Whereas Husserl's aim was to describe the essential features of consciousness which are shared by all human beings, the aim of the Geneva critics is to identify, and also to identify oneself with the consciousness of the author. A conspicuous tendency of most of these critics is to put together widely separated passages within a single work. For example, J. Hillis Miller says in his book on Charles Dickens, that all these passages "reveal the persistence of certain obsessions, problems, and attitudes" (qtd. Abrams, 225). So the critic may, in analyzing them, "glimpse the original unity of a creative mind". Besides this, the critics of consciousness often treat a single work not as an individual entity, but as part of the collective body of an author's writings in order to identify what persists through all his novels as a view of the world which is unique and the same. For phenomenological criticism, the language of a literary text is little more than an 'expression' of its inner meaning.

Husserl believes that the meaning predates language, but the poststructuralist thinking does not appreciate this viewpoint. The question is: How can one see something clearly without the conceptual resources of language at one's disposal? To this question, Husserl's philosophical theory does not give answer. The contemporary thinking is that we can only have meanings and experiences because we have a language in which we can have them. And language as a cultural construct, along with other socio-historic factors, fashions the human subject. This is a premise which is opposed to the Descartian formulation ("I think, therefore I am") upon which Husserl's theoretical edifice is built. Again, the phenomenological critics treat a single text of an author, or even some extracts from a text as representative of the author's consciousness, which may be fallacious as it does not take into account the scope for change.

We may conclude with the observation that the influence of this criticism of consciousness or phenomenological criticism reached its height in the 1950s and 1960s. Then it gave way to the explicitly opposed critical theories of structuralism and deconstruction. However, many of its concepts and procedures survive in some forms of Reader-response Criticism and Reception Aesthetics.

Works Cited

Abrams, M.H. and Geoffrey Galt Harpham. *A Handbook of Literary Terms*. New Delhi: Cengage Learning, 2009.

Habib, M.A.R. *A History of Literary Criticism*. Oxford: Blackwell Publishing, 2005, Indian Reprint, 2006.

Husserl, Edmund. "Pure Phenomenology, Its Method and Its Field of Investigation", Inaugural Lecture at Freiburg imBreisgau, 3 May 1917, tr. Robert Welsh Jordan. http://lamar.colostate.edu/~rwjordan/W-INAUGFRB.HTML accessed 20 July 2013.

Eagleton, Terry. *Literary Theory: An Introduction*. Second Edition. New Delhi: Maya Blackwell, 2000.

15

Reader-response Theory

Reader-response criticism began in the 1960s and 1970s and gained prominence in the 1980s. It had its roots in phenomenology as expounded by Edmund Husserl, Martin Heidegger, etc. The reader-response theory was largely a reaction against the new criticism, or the Formalist approach. Formalism takes a literary piece as an art object with an existence of its own, independent of, or at least, not necessarily related to its author, readers, and history of the time period during which it was written. It lays emphasis on the text, finding all meaning and value in it only. The formalists do not assign any value to the act of interpretation by the reader.

The reader-response critics, on the other hand, feel that readers have been ignored in discussions of the reading process. There is no doubt about it that some critics are primarily interested in the way a reader receives and understands literature. They believe that the reader actively contributes something to the text. In fact, reader-response critics go to the extent of saying that a text does not even exist, in a sense, until it is read by some reader. It is like the idea conveyed by the Hindi proverb *Jangal men mor naacha kisne dekha?* ('Who saw the peacock dancing in the woods?', which means reality will not be accepted unless it is perceived by the perceiver.) In case of a literary piece, it is readers who give it a meaning.

However, it has to be kept in mind that those who give an important place to readers and their responses in interpreting a work come from a number of **different critical schools**. The reader-response critics criticize formalist critics for refusing readers a place in the reading-interpretive process. According to Jane Tompkins, "reader-response critics are willing to share their critical authority with less tutored readers" (223). At the same time, they draw upon a number of theories and interpretive models based upon structuralism, psychoanalysis, phenomenology, etc.

Reader-response ideas were present in critical writings as long back as the 1920s, especially in the work of I.A. Richards, who published his book *Practical Criticism*, based primarily upon responses from the students of his class to different poems which did not show the author's name. There were a few literary figures like D.W. Harding, Walker Gibson, and Lousie Rosenblatt who were the heralds of the new movement. But it is not until the 1960s that the reader-response criticism gained enough advocates to launch an attack on the formalists.

The following are the **key ideas** of the reader-response criticism. First, in literary interpretation, the text is not the most important component, rather it is the reader who matters. In fact, there is no text unless there is a reader and the reader is the only one who can say what the text is. In a sense, the reader creates the text as much as the author does. So the critics should reject the autonomy of the text and concentrate on the reader and the reading process, as also on the interaction that takes place between the reader and the text. Another special feature of reader-response theory is that it is based on rhetoric, the art of persuasion, which has a long tradition dating back to the Greeks. The Greeks originally used it in oratory and its avowed purpose was to move the audience the way the speaker wanted. Rhetoric now refers to many types of devices or strategies used to get the reader respond to the literary work in certain ways. Wayne Booth was among the earliest of critics to give prominence to the reader in the interpretive process. He called rhetoric "the author's means of controlling his reader" (xiii).

Wolfgang Iser (1926-2007) was a German critic who applied the philosophy of phenomenology to the interpretation of literature in his *The Act of Reading: A Theory of Aesthetic Response* (1978). His approach is built on the basic distinction between the 'schematized aspects' provided by the text and the way the reader 'actualises' or 'realises' it in his mind. Phenomenology stresses the perceiver's role in any perception, that is, the role of the reader in the reading process. This philosophy aims at 'bracketing' or keeping aside all pre-suppositions while trying to capture the author's consciousness. However, Iser asserts the difficulty of separating anything from the mind that knows it. According to Iser, the critic should not explain the text as an object but its effect on the reader. He also regards the text as a central part of interpretation. Reader's experiences will govern the effect the text produces on them. Moreover, Iser says, a text does not tell readers everything; there are gaps and blanks. Readers must fill them in and thereby assemble the meanings. Iser's term of the 'blank' refers to the 'phenomenon of expectation' stimulated by the text and "filled by the reader. This principle can be applied to the elementary level of the sentence a well as to more complex units of meaning.... The reader attempts to complement what is missing through his own imagination" (Klarer, 93). Thus, they become co-authors in a sense. In his essay "The Reading Process: A Phenomenological Approach" (1972), he remarks:

> ...in reading, there are these two levels—the alien 'me' and the real, virtual 'me'—which are never completely cut off from each other. Indeed, we can only make someone else's thoughts into an absorbing theme of ourselves, provided the virtual background of own personality can adapt to it. Every text we read draws a different boundary within our personality, so that the virtual background (the real 'me') will take on a different form, according to the theme of the text concerned. (203)

Iser refers in his essay to the Polish critic **Roman Ingarden** (1893-1970), upon whose formulations he built the edifice of his theory. Ingarden, in his *The Literary Work of Art* (1931), had made the crucial distinction between the ontological nature of a text and the epistemological activity required by the reader to realize or concretize the text. According to Ingarden, the text contains layers of syntax, semantics, sound, setting and characters which do not exist unless they are realized by the reader. The actualization process is admittedly subjective.

Among other critics, the American critic **Stanley Fish** (b. 1938) has also made great contribution to the reader-response theory through the introduction of affective stylistics approach and the concept of interpretive community. He sees the reader as the text's true producer. He calls his technique of interpretation 'affective stylistics'. Like other reader-oriented critics, Fish rebels against the rigidity and dogmatism of the new critics. He thinks that the reader's activities should be "the center of attention, where they are regarded not as leading to meaning but as having meaning" (23). Fish acknowledges that the intended reader that he has in mind is the "reader whose education, opinions, concerns, linguistic competences...make him capable of having the experience the author wished to provide" (27). Fish is of the opinion that readers actually create a piece of literature as they read it. He concludes that every reading results in a new interpretation that comes about because of the strategies that readers use. As a variety of readers read a text from different perceptions, it seems reasonable to say that there may be more than one response or interpretation of the work of literature.

Affective stylistics focusses on the idea that a literary text comes into being as it is read, rather something that exists in space. It is not an objective, autonomous entity as it does not have a fixed meaning independent of the readers. The reader examine the text often line by line, even word by word, in order to understand how (stylistics) it affects (affective) the reader in the process of reading. Affective stylistics is not a description of the reader's impressionistic responses but a cognitive analysis of the material processes produced by specific elements in the text. In fact, it is a slow-motion process of analyzing how the text structures the reader's response for which affective stylistics is best known.

To summarize, at least two key features characterize different types of reader-response criticism practised by critics. One is the relegation of the text to a secondary place, giving the reader primary importance. Thus, the reader-response criticism attacks the authority of the text. This is where interpretation becomes subjective—a common charge leveled against reader-response theory. In fact, a common cause of conflict among the phenomenological critics is the fine line of distinction between 'objective' and 'subjective' interpretation by an author. In some cases, the reader can also be accused of misreading if there is no clear understanding of the role played by the text vis-à-vis the one that is played by the reader. The second feature is the study of the effect of the literary work on the reader, i.e. how does the work affect—the reader, and what strategies or devices (moral, philosophical, psychological, rhetorical) have come into play in the production of those effects? This is also the area where differences are seen among the practitioners of the theory.

Reader-response theory is also likely to appear to many people to be both esoteric. There is no doubt that readers had been given little importance in new criticism. But in spite of the potential dangers of subjectivism and esotericism, Reader-response criticism has acted as a corrective to the formalist and such other critical approaches. It seems appropriate and in keeping with the spirit of the times that the reader is given his due place in the interpretation of literature.

Works Cited

Abrams, M.H. and Geoffrey Galt Harpham. *A Handbook of Literary Terms*. New Delhi: Cengage Learning, 2009.

Booth, Wayne C. *The Rhetoric of Fiction*. Chicago: University of Chicago Press, 1961. Second edition, 1983.

Clarer, Mario. *An Introduction to Literary Studies*, New York: Routledge, 1999.

Culler, Jonathan. *Structuralist Poetics*. London: Routledge, 1975, Indian Reprint, 2012.

Fish, Stanley. "Is There a Text in This Class?" *Literature in the Reader: Affective Stylistics*. Cambridge, Mass.: Harvard University Press, 1980.

Iser, Wolfgang. "The Reading Process: A Phenomenological Approach". *Modern Criticism and Theory: A Reader*. Eds. Lodge David and Nigel Wood. Essex: Pearson, 1988, second edition 2000.

Tompkins, Jane P. *Reader-Response Criticism: From Formalism to Post-Structuralism*. Baltimore: John Hopkins University Press, 1980.

16

Reception Theory

Reception theory, like reader-response criticism, focuses on the reader's reception of a text. However, its main interest is not on the response of a single reader at a given time, but on the varying responses of the general reading public over a period of time. They re-inscribe the position of the reader in the interpretive process by investigating the manner in which the reader 'receives' the literary texts and the three entities—text, readers and society interact between themselves. It is an interdisciplinary school of criticism which draws upon fields as diverse as aesthetics, semiotics, psychology and philosophy. Most of the theorists of this school were based in Germany where the theory called *Rezeptionkritik* evolved. **Hans Robert Jauss** (1921-97), an important critic, tries to achieve a compromise between Russian formalism which ignores history, and social theories which ignore the text. Writing during a period of social unrest of the 1960s, Jauss and others wanted to question the old canon of German literature. The other critics include Hans Norbert Fugen, Rainer Warning, Harold Weinrich, Karlheinz Stierle and Hans Ulrich Gumbrecht.

Like reader-response theorists, Jauss was **opposed to Formalism and Marxism,** though he retained the formalists' stress on perception as a means in itself, and the Marxists' stress on history. He explains his position in his brilliant work *Toward an Aesthetic of Reception* (1982). The stress is on the text providing a certain stimulus and the reader completing the process. It is a form of give-and-take, a dialogue between the text and the reader. Such criticism depends heavily on the reviews in newspapers, magazines, and journals and on personal letters for evidence of public reception. The aesthetic of reception, according to Jauss, "shifts the critic's attention away from the producer of the text and from the text itself toward a dialectic of production and consumption. The history of literature becomes a crucial element in literary criticism because it allows us to comprehend the historical determiners of our understanding" (Lernout, 798).

Jauss, who was greatly influenced by the phenomenology of Husserl, uses the term **'horizon of expectations'** to describe the criteria which the readers use to judge literary texts like an epic, a tragedy, or a novel. It is a term based on several German traditions. In Jauss's reckoning, it judges what is to be regarded as poetic or literary as opposed to unpoetic or non-literary uses of languages. Ordinary writing and reading will work within such a horizon. For example, if we consider the English Augustan period, we might say that Pope's poetry was judged according to the criteria which were based upon values of clarity, naturalness and stylistic decorum. By decorum, they meant the choice of matching words to describe or narrate the content. However, it does not establish once and for all the value of Pope's poetry. During the second half of the eighteenth century, commentators began to question whether Pope was a poet at all. Some critics even suggested that he was only a clever versifier who put prose into rhyming couplets. He was accused of lacking the imaginative power required of true poetry. Omitting the next century, we can say that modern readings of Pope work within a changed horizon of expectations. We now often value his poems for their wit, a kind of morality and classicism as the eighteenth-century poets understood it.

The original concept of 'horizon of expectations' only tells us how the work was valued and interpreted when it appeared, but does not establish its ultimate meaning. In Jauss's view, it would be equally wrong to say that a work is universal, that its meaning is fixed forever and open to all readers in any period. A literary work is not an object which stands by itself and which reveals the same face to each reader in every period. It is not a monument which reveals its timeless essence in a monologue. This means, of course, that we will never be able to survey the successive horizons which flow from the time when a work was produced down to the present. To do so would be to ignore our own historical situation. The first readers may have been incapable of seeing the revolutionary significance of the writer, but the same objection must also apply to succeeding readers, including us.

Jauss's stand with regard to these objections is based upon the notion of **'hermeneutics'** as propounded by Hans-Georg Gadamer, follower of Heidegger. 'Hermeneutics' was a term originally applied to the interpretation of sacred texts; its modern equivalent preserves the same serious and reverent attitude towards the texts to which it tries to gain access. Gadamar argues that all interpretations of past literature arise from a dialogue between past and present. Our attempt to understand a work will depend on the questions which our own cultural environment allows us to raise. At the same time, we seek to discover the questions which the work itself was trying to answer in its own dialogue with history. Our present perspective always involves a relationship with the past, but at the same time the past can only be grasped through the limited perspective of the present. Moreover, the views at present are bound to be multiple. That might appear to be a hopeless scenario but a hermeneutical notion of 'understanding' does not separate knower from the object and views understanding as a 'fusion' of past and present. This means we cannot make our journey into the past without taking the present with us.

Following Gadamer's formulations, Jaussre presents tradition as a continuing 'dialogue' between a text and the ever-altering horizons of successive readers. In itself, a literary text possesses no fixed meanings. This mode of studying literary reception as a dialogue, or fusion of horizons has a double aspect. As a reception aesthetic, it defines the meaning and aesthetic qualities of any individual text as a set of semantic and aesthetic potentialities, which means the text has an aesthetic scope. These become manifest only when these are realized by the cumulative responses of readers over a period of time. In its other aspect, as a reception history, this mode of study also transforms the history of literature. Traditionally, this history was viewed as an account of the successive production of a variety of works with relatively fixed meanings—by making it a history. It requires to be told because it narrates the changing yet cumulative way that selected texts are interpreted and assessed, as the horizons of successive generations of readers alter over the passage of time.

Jauss recognizes that a writer may affront the **prevailing expectations** of his or her day. Indeed, reception theory itself developed in Germany during the 1960s in a climate of literary change. Writers like Rolf Hochhuth, Hans Magnus Enzensbeger and Peter Handke were challenging formalism through an increasingly direct involvement of readers or audience. Jauss himself examines the case of Baudelaire whose *Les Fleurs du mal* created uproar and attracted legal prosecution. It offended the norms of bourgeois morality and the canons of romantic poetry. However, the poems also immediately produced a new aesthetic horizon of expectations. The literary *avant-garde* saw the book as a trail-blazing work of decadence. In the later nineteenth century, the poems were 'concretised' as expressions of the cult of nihilism. Jauss assesses later psychological, linguistic, and sociological interpretations of Baudelaire's poems, but often disregards them. Thus, he recognizes its own historical limitations but still dubs certain other interpretations as 'illegitimate questions'. It seems the 'fusion of horizons' is not a total merging of all the points of view but only those which appear to be part of the gradually emerging totality of meanings.

Another critic **David Bleich** shows, on the basis of class room experiments, that any so-called objective reading of a literary piece is finally determined by personality of the author. It is clear from this that psychology too has a big role in deciding the reading process in which the reader is involved. Therefore, **Norman Holland** came up with the transactional theory. Herefers to the Freudian concepts of psychoanalytic criticism. His conclusion is that the literary piece provides the ground for the projection of fantasies of the author. These fantasies depend upon the personality of the author, his unconscious needs and desires. The reader's personality is likewise built of these psychological elements. When the reader reads the text, there takes place a transaction between the fantasies of the author and those of the reader, who will absorb the fantasies needed according to his 'identity theme' and create a 'meaningful totality' for himself. The concept of 'identity theme' is explained as a fixed understanding of self-inherited at birth from one's mother. However, as Guerin et al. point out, "Holland's theory, for all of its emphasis on readers and their psychology, does not deny or destroy the independence of the text" (358).

Stanley Fish (b. 1938), although associated with the reader-response theory in a big way, took the line of Reception theory in his later writings like *Is There a Text in This Class?* (1980). Towards this end, he introduced the concept of interpretive communities—a notion comprising bodies of readers who share a particular way of reading. This mode of reading may depend upon common assumptions and ways of reading of such community. Fish reposes faith in the readers by observing that they play a creative role in the process of reading. They are supposed to be well-informed; their prior experience of study of literature in general along with their life experience contribute to reader's expectations. Therefore, each reading could be a new reading and a newer interpretation. But by applying common assumptions and strategies, the readers show their belongingness to an interpretive community. Fish is conscious of the practical difficulty in cases where each member of such community comes up with his or her own interpretation and in the process constitutes "texts, intentions, speakers, and authors." How can any one know whether such a reader belongs to the same community or not. Any evidence brought forward to support the claim would itself be an interpretation. Fish observes, "The only 'proof' of membership is fellowship, the nod of recognition from someone in the same community, someone who says to you what neither of us could ever prove to a third party: 'we know.' I say it to you now, knowing full well that you will agree with me (that is, understand) only if you already agree with me" (305). An ambivalence is clearly seen here.

The reception theory continued to rule the roost in Germany in the 1970s but the English-speaking world came to know of it only when some seminal texts were translated into English in the next decade, i.e. 1980s. **Critics of other denominations** have also drawn inspiration from it, as for example, the feminists. Thus, Judith Fetterley, in her *The Resisting Reader: A Feminist Approach to American Fiction* (1978) studies the effect which particular texts have on women. Another feminist critic Patrocinio Schweickart, in her essay "Reading Ourselves: Toward A Feminist theory of Reading" (1986) rues the fact that women have been taught to read like men only and demands that gender be taken into account when the position of readers is discussed. Similarly, critics like Jonathan Culler, Norman Holland, Michael Riffaterre and Gerald Prince show the influence of the reception theory in varying degrees in their criticism.

The theory has been criticized for giving preference to the consumption of the text as against its production. The theory works on the basis of 'implied reader' but there is no clear idea of the reader here. Therefore, this theory has been criticized for being subjective and over-optimistic about the caliber of the reading public, which is bound to be composed of people of different educational, economic and socio-cultural backgrounds.

Works Cited

Fish, Stanley. "Interpreting the Variorum". *Modern Criticism and Theory: A Reader*. Eds. Lodge David and Nigel Wood Essex: Pearson, 1988, second edition 2000.

Guerin, Wilfred L. et al. *A Handbook of Critical Approaches to Literature*, fifth edition. New Delhi: Oxford University Press, 2006.

Lernout, Geert. "Reception Theory", *John Hopkins Guide to Literary Theory & Criticism*. Second Edition. Eds. Groden, Michael et al. Baltimore: The John Hopkins University Press, 2005.

17

Existentialism

Jean Paul Sartre seems to have adopted the term 'existentialism' from the French Philosopher Gabriel Marcel. He discussed his own existentialist position in a lecture in Paris on October 29, 1945 and is still regarded as a seminal document on this philosophy. The lecture was published as "Existentialism is a Humanism". The term is applied to the work of a number of philosophers since the 19th century, who generally focused on the condition of human existence, the nature of free will, an individual's responsibilities, the meaning and purpose of life, etc. The philosophy highlights the dilemma of human life in which one experiences unlimited desires, though his physical capacity is limited. Thus, a self-transcending consciousness encased in a finite physical world is the core issue of existentialism.

The early 19th century Danish philosopher **Soren Kierkgaard** (1813-55) is regarded as the father of existentialism, though he never used the term 'existentialism'. It may seem that an existentialist would necessarily be an atheist. In this respect, Kierkegaard's position needs to be ascertained. He was known to be a Christian and he did not deny that God existed, nor that humans were God's creation. But he maintained that a belief in God could only be a belief and a belief is an article of faith which is related to passion and not to a logical deduction. For him, there was an "infinite abyss" between the human and God. God had left us in "absolute isolation", which his disciple

Sartre later called abandonment. When man calls out to God, he is greeted by a massive silence. For Kierkgaard, that silence is God's presence. We are like jetsam and flotsam left on the sandy beach, and the roar of the receding tide is like the silence of God! If God has abandoned us, then it follows that we enjoy full freedom and that we are responsible for our actions. Now, this thought of being totally free and responsible at the same time leads to 'fear and trembling' for Kierkgaard (the title of his book published in 1843) and for Sartre, it provokes anguish.

The German philosopher **Friedrich Nietzsche** (1844-1900) also shows inclination for the existentialist doctrine. He was an atheist and is known for having pronounced the death of God in our times—killed in the hearts of men by science and rationalism. Mankind has tried to fill up the vacuum by raising the authority of reason or nature to that of God. He questioned religion in a radical way in his *Thus Spoke Zarthustra* (1885, trans. 1896). He rejected all metaphysical conceptions of God and heaven and wanted to affirm faith in life instead. He maintained that the individual is solely responsible for giving his/her own life meaning and for living that life passionately and sincerely, in spite of despair, angst, absurdity, alienation, and boredom. The tragic hero in literature is to be praised for affirming life in the face of all absurdity and meaninglessnesss. Man must, therefore, rise to become what he called 'overman' or superman. Such a superman has a creative will to construct meaning in life where others fail to do so. Nietzsche called this will the 'will to power'. This is not merely the power to rule over others but to rule over oneself also and that means being governed by reason.

Though both Kierkgaard and Nietzsche were considered fundamental to existential movement, they never used the term 'existentialism'. They focused on the subjective human experience rather than the objective truths of mathematics and science. Like Pascal, they were interested in people's quiet struggle with the apparent meaninglessness or purposelessness of life and the use of making free choices, particularly regarding fundamental values and beliefs, and how such choices change the nature and identity of the chooser.

In the 20th century, the German philosopher **Martin Heidegger** (1889-1976), who was influenced by Kierkegaard and Nietzsche and was a student of Husserl, developed existential phenomenology. Simone de Beauvoir was his lifelong companion. Besides, he influenced philosophers like Sartre, Camus, Gadamer, Adorno and many more. Heidegger, in his book *Being and Time* (1927), presents an analysis and solution of the problem of existence. He tried to examine what kind of 'being' was possessed by human beings. He called it *Dasein*, which literally means 'being-there' or 'being-in-the-world'. To him, human being was the only 'being' who could 'exist'. Heidegger believed that the individual was threatened by the world of things around us, his daily routine and the shallow behaviour of the crowd. The feeling of *angst* or dread brings out the 'authenticity' in us. Thus, Heidegger is responsible for propounding the concept of 'authentic existence', which means living life on one's own terms, without taking any cue from religion or other social codes. What normally happens is that most people live in 'bad faith'; they blame circumstances or God for their predicament knowing full well that they alone are responsible for all that they do. He also disapproved of any addiction to escape to an imaginary world because man can transcend even himself.

Jean Paul Sartre (1905-80), in his book *Being and Nothingness* (1943) used the famous phrase "Existence precedes essence", which forms the central reference point of this philosophy. This is explained as meaning that subjectivity must be the starting point of philosophy. The human individual is the central concern of all metaphysical thinking. According to Sartre, every human being is free to create his essence in every moment through his choices and actions. It reverses the traditional view that essence, the nature of a thing, comes before its existence, which is reflected in French philosopher Rene Desacartes' (1596-1650) famous phrase "I think, therefore I am (exist)". With that assertion, Descartes moved consciousness to the centre stage. But existentialists hold that the human being, through his consciousness, creates his own values and determines a meaning for his life. To start with, the human being does not possess any inherent identity or value. At the same time, his actions bring about consequences for which he must be ready. His actions are followed by humanity at large, therefore he must act with a sense of responsibility which is "consciousness of being the incontestable author of an event or of an object" (Sartre 553). Living authentically is not just availing of unlimited freedom from taboos and mores, but bearing a great burden also.

We might say that in case of the artifacts, essence does precede existence. Take, for example, the invention of a sword. Here the idea or the essence of the thing precedes the actual creation or the existence of the object. We also tend to put value on the object on the basis of its proximity to the idea and how well it functions. The sword that does not cut is off no use and need not be called a blade. According to Sartre, the Western philosophical tradition starting from Socrates has dealt similarly with humans. Perhaps it is thought that there is some Platonic essence that creates individual humans like a moulding machine and this idea to create humans existed in God's mind. Likewise, the humans are evaluated in terms of their correspondence to their essence. A human who does not meet the pre-established criterion is a bad human, or perhaps not a human at all. But for Sartre, all this ended in the nineteenth century when Nietzsche announced that 'God is dead'. If there is no God, there is no idea in God's mind to which the human must correspond.

Two of the first **literary authors** important to existentialism were the Czech Franz Kafka and the Russian Fyodor Dostoyevsky. Dostoyvesky's "Notes from Underground" portrays a man unable to fit into society and unhappy with the identities he creates for himself. Sartre in his book *Existential is a Humanism* quoted Dostoyvesky's *The Brothers Karamzov* as an example of existential crisis. Other novels of Dostoyvesky covered issues raised in existential philosophy. For example, in *Crime and Punishment*, the protagonist Raskolnikov experiences an existential crisis and then moves forward to Christian orthodox worldview. In the first decades of the twentieth century, a number of philosophers and writers explored existentialist ideas. Gabriel Marcel long before the coining of the term 'existentialism', introduced important existential themes to a French audience in his early essay "Existence and Objectivity" (1925) and in *Metaphysical Journal* (1927).

Following the Second World War, existentialism became a well-known and significant philosophical and cultural movement. This was because of the prominence of Sartre and Albert Camus. Sartre dealt with existential themes in his novel *Nausea* (1938) and his collection of short stories *The Wall* (1939), and his plays *The Flies* (1943) and *In Camera* (1946). But in the two years following the liberation of Paris from the German occupation, Sartre, Camus, Simone de Beauvoir, et al. became internationally famous as the leading figures of Existentialism. By the end of 1947, Camus' earlier fiction and plays had been reprinted. His new play *Caligula* had been performed and his novel *The Plague* published. His works defined and contributed to the philosophical concept of the 'absurd'. He wrote several works with existential themes including *The Rebel*, *The Stranger*, *The Myth of Sisyphus* and *Summerin Algiers*. Beauvoir's novel *The Blood of Others* was also published during this period.

While admirers of existentialism like Simone de Beauvoir say that "Existentialism is not a doctrine of despair. It is a message of hope" (Allen 77), critics of existentialism claim that the writings of existentialists are full of exaggerations. Kierkegaard's whole attitude seems morbid and unhealthy, and the same charge has been made against other existentialists. Herbert Marcuse criticized Existentialism, especially Sartre's *Being and Nothingness* (1943) for projecting anxiety and meaninglessness onto the nature of existence itself. In *Jargon of Authenticity*, Theodor Adorno criticized Heidegger's philosophy, especially his use of language, as a mystifying ideology of advanced, industrial society, and its power structure.

Works Cited

Allen, E.L. *Existentialism from Within*. London: Routledge and Kegan Paul, 1953.

Sartre, Jean-Paul. *Being and Nothingness*, tr. H.E. Barhes. London: Methuen, 1957.

18

New Historicism

New Historicism has to be differentiated from the historical approach to the study of literature which had been in existence since John Dryden (1631-1700) who tried to establish that literature in different periods of history was bound to be different and therefore, Elizabethan Drama and the Restoration Drama were to be governed by different literary conventions. The new approach to the study of history-based literature was evident in the 1970s, as in the case of J.W. Lever's study of the Jacobean Drama published in 1971. However, it was Stephen Greenblatt (b. 1943), who used the term 'New Historicism' in 1982, in the introduction to *Genre* devoted to the Renaissance literature. Important critics belonging to the area of New Historicism are Hayden White, Stephen Greenblatt, Clifford Geertz, Louis Montrose, etc.

Interestingly, the advocates of new historicism do not label their approach as a theory. They consider it as a **method** that is based upon parallel reading of literary and non-literary texts, usually of the same historical period. In other words, it is a mode of study in which literary and non-literary texts are given equal weight and constantly interrogate each other. American critic Louis Montrose defines it "as a combined interest in 'the textuality of history, the historicity of texts'. It involves (in Greenblatt's words) 'an intensified willingness to read *all* of the textual traces of the past with the attention traditionally conferred on literary texts'" (Barry, 172).

New historicism derives its origin from **dissatisfaction with structuralism** which found the world as an ordered and systematized affair. Hegel's explanation of the world on the basis of thesis, anti-thesis and synthesis could not satisfy the poststructuralists, who followed Jacques Derrida's famous formulation that 'nothing is outside the text.' The new historicists, therefore, saw the literary text as just another discourse in the array of different discourses—religious, political, economic, aesthetic. All history comes to us couched in language and if language is unstable and prone to multiple interpretations, then history itself becomes uncertain and open to myriad explanations. It is after all, "word of the past that replaces the world of the past" (Barry 175).

In this context, the impact of **Michel Foucault** (1926-84) on new historicism cannot be underrated. He advanced the fault line by elaborating the concept of discourse which was powerful enough to control thoughts of the people so that there was no scope left for any deviant thinking. If still someone did so, he was promptly dubbed as mad. M.H. Abrams remarks that "the particular discursive formations of an era determine what is at the time accounted to be 'knowledge' and 'truth', as well as what is considered to be humanly normal as against what is considered to be criminal, or insane, or sexually deviant" (190). Foucault saw the state as a tyrannical establishment that ruthlessly snooped on its subjects and controlled their thoughts through discursive practices.

New historicism, being opposed to oppressive discursive practices, is always **anti-establishment**. It is on the side of liberal ideals of personal freedom and accepts all forms of difference. New historicism, one must mention, shows an aversion to the concept of essential human nature. Even the author was not a free and autonomous individual possessing a unified personality. He, as well as the reader, were all subjects fashioned by the ideological formations of their times. Similarly, a historian writes against the backdrop of contemporary social norms and is always aware of its needs. This consideration too moulds his thinking.

On the other hand, there were also doubts expressed regarding the possibility of recovering the past through texts completely because of the time gap. How could one living so far away in terms of time from the ancient authors know them because the lifestyle, values, social systems and civilizational patterns had changed:

> How, for example, can students fed on the epistemological fat of a New Critical diet begin to appreciate the world of the Homeric epics, the language of which we are not even sure how to pronounce, and the actions of whose characters are, by our moral standards, often bizarre? How can we avoid imposing our own cultural prejudices, not mention our own interests and motives, on texts historically removed from us? (Habib, 761)

The old attitude of placing literature at a higher pedestal than the history which was taken to provide only setting was discarded. Also the **democratic** tendencies of our times also inform new historicism as these discount the rulers like kings and queens as the only befitting subject matter for history which is now taken to belong to ordinary people as well and whose records as dairies or other non-literary texts are accorded equal weightage. Instead of serving as mere contexts, the historical record is now considered co-text. New historicism also believes that all texts are products of their respective historical contexts, i.e. social, political and economic conditions which serve dominant groups and institutions. Therefore, new historicism does not merely depend upon the traditional sources for the writing of history like court records, archeological evidence, etc. It also focusses on extra-literary material like letters, diaries, films, paintings, etc. to supplement, corroborate or contradict the official versions of history. Literary texts reflect, refract, reinforce or subvert historical contexts, therefore other texts (being cultural forms) have to be studied alongside.

Turning to the critics of this school, we find that **Hayden White** (b. 1928), the most prominent new historicist and

American deconstructionist, asserted that all historical facts are turned into linguistic narratives by the historian. It is the historian who joins different historical facts and events, and tries to show them as following a logical pattern even if it might not be there. The reason is that it is human nature to try to understand developments on the basis of logic. What the historian gets are scattered facts at the most, and what he churns out is a whole story. It is not mimetic or representational in the true sense; rather it is a concoction consisting of a chronicle or time frame, a story, a mode of emplotment or plot-making, a mode of argument, and finally, an ideological base. The historian selects, combines and explains the facts in a narrative form in which all types of literary devices like metaphors, metonymy, irony, etc. are used.

Theorists like Fredric Jameson and Jean Francois Lyotard have had major influence on thought. The 'culture' in which new historicism situated literary-texts was itself regarded as a textual construct. Hence, new historicism refused to accord any kind of unity to history or culture. It viewed both as harbouring networks of contradictory, and competing forces and interests. Also it found no merit in the conviction of the new critics that literatureas an autonomous entity stood for harmony which was brought about in a literary text. Instead, it was pointed out that the apparent harmony actually hid unresolved conflicts of power involving the marginalized sections.

Some of the examples of the application of new historicism to literature include **Louis Montrose's** essay "*A Midsummer Night's Dream* and the Shaping Fantasies of Elizabethan Culture: Gender, Power, Form" (1986), in which he focusses upon the cult of the 'virgin queen' that was in circulation during Elizabethan times through texts like Spenser's *The Faerie Queen*. Montrose juxtaposes several texts of this type which depict the unbridled power of the queen along with her maiden image. But the resolution of the tensions in the Shakespearean play happens only in the patriarchal stability which was practised at that time. What Montrose drives at is the founding principle of new historicism, namely history is textualized and text is historicized and that literature also contributes to the prevailing culture by which it is inspired.

The practice of giving equal weight to **literary and non-literary material** is the first major difference between the 'New' and 'Old Historicism' also known as the historical criticism. As a representative of old historicism, we could cite E.M.W. Tillyard's *Shakespeare's History Plays* (1944). According to Tillyard, these plays reflect the Elizabethan outlook—conservative mental attitudes to society, to the deity, to the created universe, etc. The new historicism is indeed a *historicist* rather than a *historical* movement, which meansit is interested in history-as-text represented, for example, in penal, medical and colonial documents. For the new historicist, the events and attitudes of the past now exist solely as writing so that writing is subjected to close analysis formerly reserved for literary texts. The period of Renaissance came in particularly for scrutiny because:

> The perceived celebration of the individual human subject in the Renaissance, where the idea of 'Man' at the centre of nature is constituted and from which stems the driving force of humanism, also made the literature of this period and the critical responses that reinforced such a view an ideal period and the critical responses that reinforced such a view an ideal object of study for the application of theories which view 'Man', power knowledge and history in very different ways. (Webster 116)

Typically, a new historicist essay will place the literary text within the 'frame' of a non-literary text. Thus, Greenblatt's main innovation, from the viewpoint of literary study, was to juxtapose the plays of the Renaissance period with the appalling colonialist policies pursued by all the major European powers of the era. Old historicism made use of historical data for the interpretation of literary texts written in a particular historical background. But new historicism involves the parallel study of literary and non-literary texts. Thus, "the relationship between literature and history is one of circulation, exchange, and negotiation rather than of reference or reflection" (Ryan, 130).

This brings a new historicist to the conclusion that no single version of a historical event, figure or fact is valid. They also find themes/motifs where power relations have been constructed or popularized or interrogated. Greenblatt examines marginalized and non-literary texts to locate marginal identities/politics.

It should be added here that new historicism really represents a significant extension of the field of literary studies. Clifford Geertz' concept of '**thick descriptions**' or close analysis of available literary or non-literary texts merits attention. Through this technique, one could arrive not only at the hidden meaning of a text but also the conventions, codes and modes of thinking embedded in it. But in 'close reading', like the approach of the new criticism, not the entire documents, but extracts are subjected to intensive scrutiny. Sometimes, a single historical text is critically analysed. So we should not expect to find the methods of new historicism greatly valued or admired by historians. It is "history for the non-historians" (Barry, 177). However, the appeal of new historicism has been considerable for a variety of reasons. Firstly, it is written in a way which is easily accessible. Secondly, the material itself is often fascinating and is fully distinctive in the context of literary studies. These essays look different from those produced by any other critical approach. Thirdly, it is less polemical and more willing to allow historical evidence its own voice.

It may be added here that in England, the agenda of the new historicists was taken over by the cultural materialists who brought about certain changes in it. Primarily, they studied texts as sites of power relations but as connecting with our times. They are also are more politically inclined; they have faith in man to change the course of history. Thereby, they lay stress on the political initiative of man.

Works Cited

Abrams, M.H. *A Handbook of Literary Terms*. New Delhi: Cengage Learning, 2009.

Barry, Peter. *Beginning Theory: An Introduction to Literary and Cultural Theory*. Manchester, UK: Manchester University Press, 1999.

Habib, M.A.R. *A History of Literary Criticism*. Oxford: Blackwell Publishing, 2005, Indian Reprint, 2006.

Ryan, Michael. *Literary Theory: A Practical Introduction*. New York: Blackwell, 1999, Indian Reprint, 2002.

Webster, Roger. *Studying Literary Theory: An Introduction* (Second Edition). London: Hodder Headline, 1996, Reprint, 2001.

19

Cultural Materialism

Cultural materialism is a term that was used first of all by British neo-Marxist critic Raymond Williams. It has been adopted by a number of other British scholars, especially those concerned with the literature of the Renaissance. There is an attempt to indicate the Marxist aspect of their mode of new historicism. This is because they believe in the Marxist view of culture as 'superstructure' which is determined ultimately by the economic 'base' or 'structure'. According to them, whatever the textuality of history, a culture and its literary products are always conditioned by the material forces and relations of production in the relevant historical era. They are particularly interested in the political significance of a literary text not only in its own time of production but also later on. The British critic Graham Holderness regards cultural materialism as the study of historical material, including literary texts, within a politicized framework. This framework includes the present socio-cultural framework which those literary texts have helped to shape.

According to Peter Barry, the term 'cultural materialism' became popular in 1985 when it was used by Jonathan Dollimore and Alan Sinfield as the subtitle of their edited collection of essays *Political Shakespeare*. They define the term as a critical method which has **four characteristics,** namely a historical context, a theoretical method, political commitment and textual analysis. The emphasis on historical context means looking at the conditions of production and reception of a text. "The emphasis on historical context 'undermines the transcendent significance traditionally attached to literary text'. Here the word 'transcendent' roughly means timeless" (Barry, 182). No doubt, Shakespeare's plays are regarded as timeless, but the aim of cultural materialism is to allow the literary text to recover its histories which the previous studies have often ignored, which means relating the play to phenomena like the oppression of thc poor, the state power and resistance to it, etc. Secondly, the emphasis on the theoretical method means bidding goodbye to liberal humanism and welcoming the theories of structuralism, post-structuralism, etc. It also means reading across various disciplines because discourses manifest themselves in different texts. Thirdly, the emphasis on political commitment signifies a break with Christian framework and absorbing the influence of Marxist and feminist perspectives related to the disadvantaged sections of society like women, homosexuals, destitutes, etc. Finally, the stress ontextual analysis refers to the attempt to critique traditional approaches and canonical texts through close readings.

When we talk about 'cultural materialism', we have to be clear about what is meant by culture as also materialism. How the process of **understanding culture** underwent change in Britain is succinctly brought out by Guerin et al: "In modern Britain, two trajectories for 'culture' developed: one led back to the past and the feudal hierarchies that ordered community in the past; here, culture acted in its sacred function as preserver of the past. The other trajectory led toward a future, socialist utopia that would annul the distinction between labor and leisure classes and make transformation of status, not fixity, the norm" (281).

Culture, according to the cultural materialists, expresses itself through different forms like movies, television, popular music, literature, etc. When they talk about literature, they do not mean only the canonical authors like Shakespeare or other literary stalwarts, rather they include in it popular literature also. By clubbing culture with materialism, they hit at all idealistic notions of culture, according to which culture is the product of enlightened and liberated minds. "Culture is not simply a reflection of the economic and political system, but nor can it be independent of it" (Dollimore and Sinfield, 3). This ambivalence is the main plank of distinction of cultural materialism from the thoroughly Marxist materialist view.

Cultural materialism is taken as having **evolved from new historicism**. Therefore, it is natural that both should share some common ground. Both believe that subjects cannot transcend the times they live in and share perspectives constructed by prevailing ideology. They go by the truism that ideology, being always political, is a vehicle for power. One cannot treat culture as independent of these conditions. There is a definite relation between human action and socio-economic formations. Literary criticism is inseparable from ideological values and biases. Feminism was also important for cultural materialists in recognizing how seemingly disinterested thought is shaped by power structures such as patriarchy. For example, a play by Shakespeare is related to the context of its production—to the economic and political system of its period. It is also found to be subject to the institutions of cultural production, i.e. the church, theatre, education system, etc.

A number of **critiques on Shakespeare** have been published by critics belonging to the cultural materialist school in the present century. In *Alternative Shakespeares* (1985) edited by John Drakakis, a number of critics challenged the liberal humanist language of character analysis, artistic coherence, and harmony. They drew attention to the manner in which Shakespeare's texts produce meaning, construct the human subject, and engage in larger ideological issues. Similarly, Alan Sinfield's edited work *Shakespeare, Authority, Sexuality* (2006) explores the inter-play of textuality, history and culture in the plays of Shakespeare and other contemporaries. The contributors particularly focus on the scope for dissidence and apply, among others, the queer theory to that period. Interestingly, the tendency to place the present alongside past known as 'presentism' is also evident in Terence Hawkes' *Shakespeare in the Present* (2002). In this work, he suggests ways to apply present materialist principles to Shakespeare. Another book in this category *Presentiest Shakespeare* (2006), co-edited by Hawkes with Hugh Grady, extends the critical norms questioning the past on the basis of the present.

Literature does not merely reflect the culture in which it is written; it also actively contributes to the constitution of culture. Like new historicism, cultural materialism shows how ideology, working through the existing social order, tries to maintain its firm grip on new circumstances which may develop with the passage of time and may be detrimental to the power of ideology. Both new historicism and cultural materialism also assign equal weight or status to different texts—literary, religious, economic, legal, etc.

When it comes to **difference** between new historicism and cultural materialism, it may be pointed out that the latter is consciously political. They not only read the texts of the past with an eye to locate the marginalized and the modes of exploitation but also look for modes of resistance and subversion. In a way, their interpretations have got to be materialistic as also political. This is so because they believe that all modes of representation are political activities which means these are meant to possess and retain power. Literary texts are sites of political struggle through which existing power structures are sought to be reinforced.

An important point of difference with new historicism relates to the Foucault's notion of discourse—an all-pervasive power that moulds the thinking of all subjects. Raymond Williams propounded the concept of 'structures of feeling' as against Foucault's conception. Williams finds these structures at variance, and at times, in conflict with the prevailing beliefs and values. He illustrates his point with the fiction of Charles Dickens whose treatment of themes showed his antipathy to the prevailing values or reigning discourse. Dollimore and Sinfield also strike one with their oft-quoted remark: "Men and women make their own history but not in conditions of their own choosing" (3). This makes cultural materialism a project full of optimism.

Then, while the new historicists place a literary text in the political situation of their own times, the cultural materialists place it in our times. That creates space for political action. Cultural materialists criticize new historicists for leaving no scope for effective action and change and for downplaying subversion and dissent. But cultural materialists are particularly interested in the political significance, especially the subversive aspects and effects of a literary text. The literary texts may, at first sight, seem to support contemporary ideology, but the cultural materialists find that the particular ideology is less persuasive in the text than what the new historicists think. Thus, the analyses of literary texts by cultural materialists bring to light how a text acts as an instrument of a dominant socio-cultural order but the critics also demonstrate inner contradictions in a text which it seeks to hide. In other words, the cultural materialists interpret texts to locate their relevance to our times and look for the scope for agency for the marginalized through its subversive potential.

Works Cited

Barry, Peter. *Beginning Theory: An Introduction to Literary and Cultural Theory*. Manchester, UK: Manchester University Press, 1999.

Guerin, Wilfred L. et al. *A Handbook of Critical Approaches to Literature*, fifth edition. New Delhi: Oxford University Press, 2006.

Dollimore, Jonathan and Alan Sinfield, eds. *Political Shakespeare: New Essays in Cultural Materialism*. Manchester: Manchester University Press, 1985.

20

Cultural Studies

Cultural studies is by no means a new phenomenon. Debates on what is meant by culture and what exactly constitutes it have been going on since the time history was first written. Starting with Plato, many thinkers and critics have expressed their views on the larger cultural issues surrounding the study of literature. But it was in the 1980s or so that cultural studies evolved into an inter-disciplinary and trans-disciplinary analytical approach. Cultural studies subsumes different critical methodologies like the British cultural materialism, American new historicism, American multi-culturism, Postmodernism and popular culture and postcolonial studies.

The new face of cultural studies started emerging with Raymond Williams' (1921-88) path-breaking works: *Culture and Society* (1958), *The Long Revolution* (1961), and *Marxism and Literature* (1977). Even Greenblatt, the other major theoretician of the new historicist school called his critical approach as 'Poetics of Culture'. Cultural studies links text, discourse and material practices. The practitioners of this kind of criticism study power relations working behind a cultural form. They go into the questions regarding its mode of production, marketing, audience, relation to genre and to other works in genre, relevance, etc.

The most conventional **definition** of the word "culture" refers to the beliefs, rituals, and practices of a given social or ethnic group or nation. More generally, the word has been used to refer to what is produced by human beings, as opposed to nature. In his "Culture and Anarchy", Matthew Arnold defined culture as "the best that has been thought and said". *The John Hopkins Guide to Literary Theory and Criticism* describes culture in the following way:

> Culture is how we live nature including our own biology; it is the shared meanings we make and encounter in our everyday lives. Culture is not something embodied in 'particular' texts (i.e., any commodity, object or event that can be made to signify); it is the practices and processes of making meanings with and from the 'texts' we encounter in everyday lives. (Storey, 220)

Since culture includes our lifestyle, beliefs, practices, taboos, knowledge, traditions, customs, norms, values, etc., the term 'cultural studies' must have a very wide scope. As an **eclectic discipline**, cultural studies is composed of elements of Marxism, poststructuralism, Lacanian psychology, Foucauldian discourse, gender studies, anthropology, sociology, ethnology, film theory, public policy, popular culture studies, postcolonial studies, etc. As applied to the study of literature, cultural criticism now includes not only the usual genres of poetry and drama, fiction but also popular fiction such as thrillers and romances, mass media, cinema, theatre, magazines, and music. Cultural criticism sees literature and literary meaning as part of a larger context that includes the ideological context of prevailing beliefs, and broad political issues of class, race, and gender, and the operations of power. Typically, cultural studies has extended its methodology to encompass field surveys, empirical observations, interviews, interdisciplinary linkages, etc.

Ronald Barthes' (1915-80) *Mythologies* (1957), which undertakes brief readings of a range of cultural activities, was a precursor of contemporary cultural studies. The activities commented upon in the text include professional wrestling, fashions, advertisement of cars and detergents, French wine and Einstein's brain. Another precursor could be the British school of neo-Marxist studies in literature and art. This movement was inaugurated by Raymond Williams' *Culture and Society*

(1958) and Richard Hoggart's (b. 1918) *The Uses of Literacy* (1958). The movement took the form of an institution with the establishment of the Centre for Contemporary Cultural Studies (BCCCS) at the University of Birmingham. It was founded in 1964 by Hoggartand in 1968. Stuart Hall took over as its director.

The Marxists viewed culture as a part of ideological process whereby the ruling class foists its own values on the rest of society. In this tradition, culture has been regarded as an instrument of dominance or oppression. The **Frankfurt school** saw modern mass culture as bland commercialism. The school was interdisciplinary, with an emphasis on cultural studies and critical theory. Leading figures of the school included Max Horkheimer, Theodor Adorno, Herbert Marcuse, Walter Benjamin and Stuart Hall, the critics belonging to this school produced analyses of modern culture, drawing on Marxist and sometimes on Freudian theory. Adorno and Horkheimer produced an incisive critique of modern culture. They argued that culture under monopoly capitalism imposes a sterile uniformity on everything: "Films, radio and magazines make up a system which is uniform as a whole and in every part" (120).

In contrast to the views of the Frankfurt School, **Marxists** such as Antonio Gramsci (1891-1937) have seen culture as an instrument of possible resistance to the prevailing ideologies. This is because of the development of a counter-culture of workingclass. While Stuart Hall's (b. 1932) work on popular culture hogged the limelight in England, in America, the Marxist critic Fredric Jameson (b. 1934) underlined the postmodern tendencies in mass culture. In Russia, the Marxist Valentin Volosinov (1895-1936) had already seen the linguistic sign as the basis for ideological and cultural struggle. Many cultural critics such as John Fiske (b. 1939) have drawn on semiotics to analyze elements of popular culture. In his *Television Culture* (1987), Fiske argues that the techniques and codes employed by television mould our perceptions. But he rejects the idea that audiences are wholly passive consumers of ideological meanings.

Different approaches under the rubric of cultural studies generally share some common ground: First, cultural studies tends to transcend the confines of a particular discipline such as literary criticism or history. It may be pointed out here that the basic approach in both cultural studies and cultural materialism is the same materialistic one, but whereas cultural materialism examines the relationship between literature and history, cultural studies includes all cultural forms and manifestations like fashion shows, exhibitions, cinema, public monuments, etc. Thus, the scope of 'text' is widened to include objects also so that there is no hierarchy of text/object formed. Greenblatt rightly calls the objects the 'textual traces of a culture'. Some of the journals like *Critical Inquiry, Representations*, etc. are devoted to the study of cultural phenomena surrounding texts, like the Italian opera, the architectural styles of prisons, body piercing, etc. In India also, increasing interest in cultural study can be seen, as for example in Pramod Nayar's *Reading Culture: Theory, Praxis, Politics* (2006) in which the writer has examined cultural forms like comics, tourism brochures and museums.

Secondly, cultural studies is politically engaged. Cultural critics see themselves in opposition to many power structures of society at large as also within the academy. They question inequalities within power structures and seek to discover models to restructure relationships between majority and minority discourses. Hence, culture is always political. In other words, we can say that culture is political because the social process examined by political analysis is always embedded in culture.

Raymond Williams' (1921-88) conception of cultural materialism went further, however. The key question was how the relationship between society and culture was understood. In his 1958 essay "Culture is Ordinary", Williams cited the Marxist tenet that "a culture must finally be interpreted in relation to its underlying system of production" and described culture as follows: "a culture is a whole way of life, and the arts are part of a social organization which economic change clearly radically affects" (95). The second part of this statement indicates Williams' resistance to the classical Marxist idea of culture as a 'superstructure' which echoes an economic 'base'. The first part suggests how he would bridge the gap: culture was "a whole way of life". Williams counterposes it to 'high culture'—"this extraordinary decision to call certain things culture and then separate them, as with a park wall, from ordinary people and ordinary work" (94).

If Williams' views did not impress all, the rise of poststructuralism in the late 1960s further erased the difference between high and low culture: "Jacques Derrida's 'deconstruction' of the world/text distinction, like all his deconstructions of hierarchical oppositions, has urged—or enabled—cultural critics "to **erase the boundaries** between high and low culture, classic and popular literary texts, and literature and other cultural discourses that, following Derrida, maybe seen as manifestations of the same textuality" (Guerin, 276).

Cultural studies, therefore, denies the separation of elite and popular culture. Being a cultured person used to mean being acquainted with highbrow art and intellectual pursuits. In different civilizations, culture had always an elitist orientation. In India too, the inculcation of sanskar or the process of acculturation has always meant imbibing lofty values and attaining scholarship through canonical texts. But the postmodern development in the West seeks to change our conventional understanding of culture. Cultural critics today take in mass culture, whether folk or urban. Cultural critics argue that after World War II, the distinctions among high, low, and mass culture collapsed. Rather than determining which are the best works produced, cultural critics probe how these works are produced and how various productions relate to one another. They aim to reveal the political, economic reasons why a certain cultural product is more valued at certain times than others.

Cultural studies is, by and large, a **materialist critique** in which the material conditions prevailing at the time of production of any cultural form including art and literature are interrogated. Just as the producer of any item goes in for strategies like attractive packaging and advertisement-based promotion of any product in the market, similarly, the cultural forms are also packaged and marketed by the promoters of culture or power structures. The way the analogy is read, it follows that culture is a subset of larger consumerism. Marxist critics have long realized the importance of such paraliterary questions as: Who supports a given artist? Who publishes his or her books, and how are these books distributed? Who buys books? For that matter, who is literate and who is not? Cultural studies thus becomes subjective—that is, culture is relation to individual lives—with a direct approach to attacking social ills.

In order to explain how culture can work as the handmaiden of the powerful, we must turn to the Italian thinker Antonio Gramsci's (1891-1937) enunciation of **'hegemony'**, which is different from the working of discourse and ideology. According to it, "a social class achieves a predominant influence and power, not by direct and overt means, but by succeeding in making its ideological views so pervasive that the subordinate classes unwittingly accept and participate in their own oppression" (Abrams, 162). It is to be differentiated by Marxist notion of ideology in which there is no scope for negotiation. Gramsci believes in the power of literature and human agency to play a positive role in bringing about change. "Gramsci learned from Marx, that we make culture and we are made by culture; there is agency, and there is structure. It is not enough to celebrate agency, nor is it enough to detail the structure(s) of power; we must always keep in mind the dialectical play between agency and structure, between production and consumption" (Storey, 222). What it means is that just as reader-consumer is faced by the structure, the text also faces the consumer and depends for meaning upon the understanding of the reader.

As mentioned above, there is no distinction made between elitist and popular cultures. **Stuart Hall** (b. 1932), who was the director of CCCS until 1979, did commendable work on popular culture. His espousal of popular culture as the central focus of cultural studies was so powerful that the critic Jim McGugan referred to the movement as 'cultural populism'—the term which he also used as the title of his book published in 1992. But Hall was never in favour of institutionalizing cultural studies or making it "an orthodoxy, a self-contained discipline or set of formal theories incapable of making political intervention" (Procter, 140). Mercifully, cultural studies has moved on to understand the questions of cultural adjustment in case of the myriad diasporas spread all over the globe. Besides, it has focused attention on racial and ethnic studies in multicultural societies.

To sum up, then, "Cultural Studies could encompass inquiries in a wide variety of fields such as sociology, anthropology, history, literature, and the arts", observes M.A.R. Habib (173). It regards literature as a set of semiotic codes among broader social codes. It views literature as an instrument of subordination or subversion—clearly a site of ideological struggle. On the other hand, it also concerns itself with the practices of everyday life of common people, like watching television or eating out. It studies the meanings peoples attribute to such practices and to various objects of use like cars and gadgets. It has an empirical, interdisciplinary, and collaborative methodology and is set to play a significant role in the globalized village that the world has become now.

Works Cited

Storey, John. "Cultural Studies", *The John Hopkins Guide to Literary Theory & Criticism*. Second Edition. Eds. Groden, Michael et al. Baltimore: The John Hopkins University Press, 2005.

Guerin, Wilfred L. et al. *A Handbook of Critical Approaches to Literature*, fifth edition. New Delhi: Oxford University Press, 2006.

Habib, M.A.R. *Modern Literary Criticism & Theory: A History*. Oxford, UK: Blackwell, 2008.

Procter, James. *Stuart Hall*. New Delhi: Routledge, 2007.

Williams, Raymond. "Culture is Ordinary", *The Everyday Reader*, Ed. Ben Highmore. London: Routledge, 2002.

Adorno and Horkheimar. "The Culture Industry: Enlightenment as Mass Deception" *Dialoectic of Enlightenment*. New York: Continuum, 2001.

21

Postcolonial Theory

The term postcolonial (with a hyphen) represents a temporal phase being experienced by those societies which suffered colonization and are now free, while the term Postcolonial (without a hyphen), in use now, connotes much more: it represents a creative mindset and a critical approach. Most of the countries in what is commonly called the Third World were colonized by one European country or the other—Britain, France, Germany, Italy, Spain, Portugal, etc. After the colonized countries of Asia, Africa, Latin America and the Caribbean got freedom through long struggles, they were obliged to re-build their ravaged nations. It was natural that the Third World writers should focus on both colonialism and its impact on cultures of their respective nations. Among the many challenges facing postcolonial writers are the resurrection of their cultures and combatting misconceptions about them.

Postcolonialism, then, is concerned with the analysis of history, culture and literature of former colonies of various European countries and the impact of colonization on them. The first step in the direction of postcolonial discourse (or the idea of postcolonialism in literature and public domain) was taken in the 1950s, when a Martinique-born poet **Aime Cesaire** (1913-2008) published his essay captioned "Discourse on Colonialism" (1955). This was responsible for the emergence of concepts like 'negritude', which aimed at resisting the Western hegemony through highlighting the cultural achievements of the coloured people.

It is well known that the Western intellectuals re-wrote the history of the native people from their standpoint, as **Albert Memmi** (b. 1920) states in his book *The Colonizer and the Colonized* (1965): "The most serious blow suffered by the colonized isbeing removed from history" (Groden 757). Actually, it was done by the colonizers to attribute to themselves a superior image and to infuse an inferiority complex in the natives whom they had defeated politically. Apart from pointing to the lapses made in this regard, postcolonialism seeks to take the academia out of this straitjacketing or closed mindset and provide it with the necessary insight to deal with the reality from an objective standpoint. That should mean mutual respect—a notion inherent in the term 'Postcolonialism' which hints at the world having moved beyond the colonial phase and the thinking tied to it.

Postcolonial theory explains the process of colonization as issuing out of the twin phenomena of modernization and industrialization, because these needed procurement of raw material and labour from outside Europe. The search for trade routes was also impelled by this need. Colonialism by various European nations began soon after the discovery of the sea-route to India and America. Economic exploitation was facilitated through military conquest or as in case of India, the politics of 'divide and rule'. During their rule, the colonial masters studied the colonized nations with the motive of culturally dominating them so as to better exploit them economically. This kind of domination required the creation of the notion of the superiority of the white race. The Western scholars intentionally represented the colonized territories as mysterious and exotic and also, at the same time, full of potential for exploitation. This was done with the intention of inviting their reluctant compatriots back home to come over to tighten their grip on the colonized. The people were portrayed as ignorant, irrational and sentimental. One finds this approach in Joseph Conrad's novel *Heart of Darkness*. The character of Dr. Aziz in E.M. Forster's *A Passage to India* is also a typical example. The existing cultural practices of the native people were represented in such works as kinds of superstition and voodoo. The postcolonial literature seeks to correct this biased approach.

Franz Fanon (1925-61) came up withhis book *The Wretched of the Earth* (1961) which analyzed the psychological and sociological factors inherent in colonialism. To him, racism was the result of colonial oppression because when the colonizer represented the native as backward, the latter began to supplant white man for the term 'man'. According to Fanon, "Colonialism is not satisfied merely with holding people in its grip and emptying the native's brain of all form and content. By a kind of perverted logic, it turns to the past of the oppressed people, and distorts, disfigures and destroys it" (169). Poststructuralist theories, with their emphasis on deconstruction and decentering, have informed the rise of postcolonial theory. This has highlighted further the ethnocentric nature of European literature, and in particular the 'Englishness' of English literature.

While the voices against the Western attempt to culturally dominate the colonized nations had been raised by Mahatama Gandhi in India, Cesaire and Franz Fanon in Africa, it was left to the Palestinian-American **Edward Said** (1935-2003) to forcefully articulate the position of the colonized in his famous work *Orientalism* (1978), which became the Bible of the postcolonial critical theory. According to him, colonialism was not only a military-cum-political project but also a cultural one. The Western colonial powers had a biased approach to the understanding of the colonized. He named this approach as Orientalism. The discourse of *Orientalism* circulated narratives about cruelty, sensuality, despotism, laziness and so on to constitute the 'Other' against which a positive identity of the colonizer could be constructed. Said viewed the postcolonial writing as a form of resistance to Orientalism. In another book *Culture and Imperialism* (1993), Said analyses the rise of colonial discourse through culture and narrative and notes that the process of subordinating the native

> ...uses narrative to dispel contradictory memories and occlude violence—the exotic replaces the impress of power with the blandishments of curiosity—with the imperial

> presence so dominating as to make impossible any effort to separate it from historical necessity. All these together create an amalgam of the arts of narrative and observation about the accumulated, dominated, and ruled territories whose inhabitants seem destined never to escape, to remain creatures of European will (159).

This was followed by **Homi K. Bhabha's** (b. 1949) concepts of hybridity, mimicry and ambivalence located in the colonial discourse which he elaborated in his book *The Location of Culture*. He suggests that the colonial authority was often subverted from the inside by the colonizer (on some occasions) and by the natives. He deals with the construction of the colonial subject in his essay "Of Mimicry and Man: The Ambivalence of Colonial Discourse" (1984). The essay is an exploration of the relations and attitudes of the colonizers and the colonized. On the one hand, the colonial discourse sought to humanize the third world native *a la* Kipling's "White Man's Burden" thesis, on the other, they did not want to humanize him fully fearing loss of hegemony. This led to the creation of a native who was partially anglicized. He was made half-English and half-native. The notion of 'hybridity' is central to Bhabha's work, according to which a state of 'in-betweenness', situates in a person who stands between two cultures: "In the ambivalent world of the 'not quite/not white', in the margins of metropolitan desire, the *founding objects* of the Western world become the erratic, eccentric, accidental objects trouves of the colonial discourse—the part-objects of presence. It is then that the body and the book [Bible] lose their representational authority" (Bhabha 92).

Another important postcolonial critic is **Gayatri Chakravorty Spivak** (b. 1941), an American professor of Indian origin. In her influential essay "Can the Subaltern Speak?" (1983), she questions whether people in subordinate, colonized positions are able to have a voice. The term 'subaltern' was used by the Italian Marxist critic Antonio Gramsci to refer to the working masses. They needed to be organized by left-wing intellectuals into a politically self-conscious force. According to M.H. Abrams, 'subaltern' is "a British word for someone of inferior rank, and combines the Latin terms for 'under' (*sub*) and 'other' (*alter*)" (238). Spivak's well-known argument is that the subaltern cannot speak for him/herself because the very structure of colonialism prevents the speaking. For the colonized woman, this is even more impossible because the double bind of colonialism and patriarchy represses her completely: "If, in the context of colonial production, the subaltern had no history and cannot speak, the subaltern as female is even more deeply in shadow" (Bertnes 212). The female subaltern simply cannot represent herself. Spivak also cautions against homogenizing and thus 'essentializing' the subject and points out that the colonized subaltern *subject* is very heterogeneous and that there cannot be any comparison in the situation of a Western woman and the one belonging to the Third World. She challenges postcolonial theory to address the silencing of women and other subaltern subjects not only by and in colonial discourses but also in postcolonial responses to those discourses.

Spivak also uses the term **'epistemic violence'** (from Foucault) which refers to the destruction of non-Western ways of knowing and resulting dominance of Western ways of understanding. Thus, the postcolonial theory focusses on the aesthetic, ideological and political aspects and analyzes the relationships between the centre and the periphery. It is through the control of the discourse that cultural imperialism is foisted and a particular human subject is created by those who wield power. In this respect, it may be pointed out that some postcolonial critics have focussed on the British literature of 18th and 19th centuries and found that colonial exploitation was at the root of the representation in literature of the social and economic life of that period.

Critical postcolonial readings regularly proceed under the **influence** of postcolonial theory. This theory raises and explores historical, cultural, political, and moral issues surrounding the establishment and disintegration of colonies and the empires which ruled over them. According to one view, postcolonial literature and theory have so far been strongly influenced by theorists primarily concerned with the Middle East and the Indian sub-continent. Many of their insights and concepts regarding postcolonial writing cannot, however, be transferred to other regions. Accordingly, it is likely that African, Caribbean, Hispanic, and Irish voices, among others, will give postcolonial literature and theory new vistas.

Later postcolonial writers have marked the colonizer-colonized matrix within the self-governed nations also, where **the centre** is likened to colonizer and those at the periphery, as for example, women and weaker sections of society are compared to the colonized. Also, the exploitation on the basis of caste, creed, sex, race and sexuality is condemned as 'internal colonization'. The postcolonial theory attempts to recover the subaltern history/literature as against those of the upper classes. In India, the focus on Dalit literature is the result of this movement.

At the same time, the very **concept of nation** has come under fire in the context of globalization and it is felt that the nation is an imaginary construct only. It is indeed surprising considering that the postcolonial theory started with the interrogation by the native people of the subjugation by colonizing foreign nations. The same natives are now supposed to question the very concept of their own nation. The advocates of the concept of nation point out that even though the differences are sacrosanct for the postcolonialists, for any collective formation such as a nation, differences have to be reconciled to a limited extent and majority principle is the only tool available for democracy. As no alternative to the idea of nation is proposed, this kind of postcolonialist stand is purely theoretical and impractical.

The postcolonial theory has also encompassed the study of different **diasporas**. While in the colonized period, forced migration of labour was common at the hands of the colonizer, after the collapse of colonization, the phenomenon of migration of economically weaker people to rich countries started. Alongside, there was migration based upon political harassment for some people who had politically antagonistic views with the establishment in their home countries. As these people migrated to alien societies, the cultural integration became a problem. This happened because the migrants were treated as 'cultural others'. Postcolonial literature is concerned with this discrimination and seeks to suggest ways to overcome the problem which is getting more and more in focus due to the transformation of the world into a global village. Homi Bhabha's concepts of hybridity, in-betweenness, liminality, etc. have come in handy for the discussion of the condition of the migrant. Diaspora studies is now treated as part of the cultural studies.

We can, thus, identify the following major issues in postcolonial criticism:

1. It is the rejection of the master-narrative of Western imperialism in which the colonial other is subordinated and marginalized, and finally, deleted as a cultural agency.
2. It seeks to dislodge Eurocentric norms of literary and artistic values, and to expand the literary canon to include colonial and postcolonial writers.
3. It shows an abiding concern with the formation of the colonial and post-colonial 'subject' and the categories by which this subject conceives itself and perceives the world around him.
4. A recurrent topic of debate is how a subaltern subject who writes in a European language can manage to challenge and fight against the very discourse that has created its subordinate identity.
5. The idea of nation has come under fire for being an imaginary community.
6. The colonizer-colonized paradigm is applied to the self-governed nations also, as in respect of suppression of the weaker sections of society.
7. Postcolonialism studies the diasporic situation of the immigrant communities and points out the unequal relationships disapproving lack of cultural space to the immigrant.

In conclusion, it can be said that postcolonialism is not a unified movement. It was a starting point only which led to the revision of Marxism and feminism. But the postcolonial theoreticians have come up with a plethora of terms and rendered theory jargon-ridden. Postcolonial theory today studies the formation of subjectivities and identities and questions the concept of nation. The postcolonialists feel that in the name of homogenizing, the centre in any society negates differences, which are humanistic traits necessary for individual identity.

Works Cited

Abrams, M.H. and Geoffrey Galt Harpham. *A Handbook of Literary Terms*. New Delhi: Cengage Learning, 2009.

Bertnes, Hans. *Literary Theory: The Basics*. Oxford: Routledge, 2001.

Bhabha, Homi K. *The Location of Culture*. London: Routledge, 1994.

Fanon, Franz. *The Wretched of the Earth*. London: Penguin, 1967, Reprint 1990.

Groden, Michael et al. eds. *The John Hopkins Gide to Literary Theory & Criticism*. Second Edition. Baltimore: The John Hopkins University Press, 2005.

Said, Edward. *Culture and Imperialism*. London: Chatto & Windus, 1993.

22

Diaspora Theory

The origin of the word 'diaspora' is from the Greek 'dia' (through) and 'speirein' (scatter). As such, it gives the sense of dispersal through space. Going into the history of its usage, we find that it was first applied to the **Jewish community**, which had been stateless since Biblical times and was spread all over the world, where it faced discrimination and oppression. The term 'Diaspora' referred to these Jews. It was only in 1949 that the present state of Israel was carved out of the Palestine territory occupied by the Allied Powers during the Second World War. This creation of the new nation has not been peaceful and even now it continues to be a major cause of conflict in West Asia.

However, the term became popular and was used in the context of **other nationalities** also which had been displaced from the original homelands due to one reason or the other. Not going far back in time, we can relate the present major diasporas to the period when certain nations of Europe became maritime powers and started the phase of colonization which led to the system of slavery whereby human beings were forcibly captured and made to work like cattle in distant colonies. The black population of America owes its origin to this inhuman practice.

When slavery was abolished by the British Government in 1833-34, France and Holland also followed suit. In its place, the system of **indentured labour** was introduced and large contingents of people were taken from colonies by the colonizers to other places where they were treated as bonded labourers. It happened in the case of Indians who were taken to far-off Mautitius, Fiji or South Africa by the ruling British to work as plantation workers. Other colonial powers like France and Portugal also took Indian workers to Surinam, Martinique, Angola, Mozambique, etc. Similarly, Indian soldiers were forcibly sent by the British rulers to fight wars on their behalf.

The past century witnessed large-scale displacement and dispersal of populations across the world as a result of **major political upheavals**—among them the two European wars, decolonization and the Cold War. Following these, globalization, spurred by free trade and increased capital flows, and new technologies of communication, information, and travel, has accelerated the movement of people, commodities, ideas, and cultures across the world. Diaspora is regarded not as a singular phenomenon but as historically varied and heterogeneous in its aspects. The transnational mobility of people may be the result of forced or voluntary migration, of self-exile or expulsion. Refugees, people in transit, are the product of war, ethnic conflict and natural calamity.

So far as we in **India** are concerned, the second wave of immigration was not under duress. Business-minded Gujarati people moved to certain African countries like Kenya and South Africa for the sake of establishing business there and created what is dubbed as the 'trade diaspora'. More recent times saw the migration of skilled and semi-skilled manpower, mainly from Kerala, to the oil-rich Sheikhdoms of the United Arab Emirates. Also professionals and entrepreneurs went to the First World countries like the UK and the USA. After a gap, this trend has picked up in our times as the third wave of migration of professionals and educated elite who have gone wherever they could find greener pastures.

All such Indians who have been living outside India constitute the Indian diaspora. The Indian diaspora, which is twenty million strong and is scattered in more than 110 countries of the world (Sharma, 19), has never stopped looking back at their homeland. When India was under the British Rule, the diaspora shaped the history of the independence movement of India. In the post-independence scenario, it has contributed to the raising of foreign currency reserves through remittances and in this they have achieved top position among all the diasporas of the world. They have also invested in economic and social uplift of the country. Of course, there is also the lunatic fringe that has been instrumental in instigating subversive movements in India but then a little chaff always comes with the grain.

Even though distinction has to be made between forced and willing movement of people, the phenomenon of diaspora necessarily involves a structure of location followed by **dislocation and relocation**. Moving away from one's homeland and settling elsewhere on a long-term basis does mean dislocation that brings in a sense of loss and nostalgia. This is followed by a bid for relocation in an alien milieu through negotiation and adjustment. And yet there is no guarantee that the outcome will be sure success; hybridity or in-betweenness being quite common here.

The diasporic communities are defined as the groups of people that are distanced from their homeland—as political or economic migrants in search of work or refugees escaping war. The experience of exile may be accompanied by a sense of belonging to the former homeland and a continued allegiance to that remembered culture while staying within the host country. As such, the diasporas can be defined as "heterogeneous cultures, spatially separated from their place of origin yet living between places in their identity and cultural life" (Hartley, 66). The stress on in-betweenness in such cases has to be underlined here. This very characteristic has been brashly put forth by Salman Rushdie in his *Imaginary Homelands*: "Sometimes we feel that we straddle two cultures; at other times, that we fall between two stools" (15).

Pointing to the common **characteristics** of the diaspora members, William Safren (quoted by Satendra Nandan) comments that they "retain a collective memory, vision or myth about their original homeland" and believe they cannot be fully accepted by their lost society and therefore feel partly alienated. At the same time, they "regard their ancestral homeland as their true, ideal home and as the place to which they or their descendents would (or should) eventually return when conditions are appropriate". They continue to relate to that homeland and also feel committed to its maintenance or restoration. As can be seen, these characteristics are not without gaps and contradictions which is a concomitant of the essentializing process that overlooks the differences in which the diaspora members live. According to Bill Ashcroft et al., "The development of diasporic cultures necessarily questions essentialist models, interrogating the ideology of a unified, 'natural' cultural norm, one that underpins the centre/margin model of colonialist discourse" (70).

It is common experience that when one, driven away from home due to economic compulsions/ambitions, has been living abroad for a long time, one feels home-sick. This is on two counts: One misses the extended family and friends back home. The time spent in the country of origin is the early part of life—childhood, adolescence, etc. when experience of life under the care of parents is positive and enjoyable. Secondly, lack of proper adjustment within the milieu of the adopted country at a stage in life when struggle is called for, makes one turn to pleasant memories of the native land. His condition is akin to what Mathew Arnold described along ago: "Standing between two worlds/one dead the other powerless to be born". In such a situation, the **bonding** of culture, religion, literature and language is especially strong among the expatriates. But whereas it provides ethnic identity and a sense of self, it can also alienate one from the host culture. It is this displacement which gives diasporic writing its peculiar sense of loss and nostalgia. Therefore, loss and nostalgia constitute key elements of any diasporic writing. At the same time, it gives vent to a certain alienation due to incomplete assimilation in the adopted society, which has much to do with factors like race and ethnicity mostly marked in body colour and features, which cannot be wished away.

Another way to look at the **diasporic writing** is to note the motifs of dislocation, homelessness, rootlessness and escape. These are the narratives of grief and joys, aspirations and helplessness. John Hartley rightly states: "The psychological and cultural experience of diaspora can be one of hybridity, exile, nostalgia, selective adaptation or cultural invention" (66). It is this experience that is sought to be transmitted to readers through the diasporic literature. It would be seen that the diaspora writers are obsessed with search for identity and their writing displays a poetics of exile and displacement. Some of the common themes of the diasporic writing focus on the linkage between the individual and his socio-cultural environment. It also stresses the importance of religion and an ethics that is based upon religion. Talking about the significance of the diasporic writing, Michael Ryan comments, "In situations of severe racial oppression like the United States and South Africa, literature came to be seen as a privileged site for understanding the social structures, cultural codes, and psychological tropes of cross-cultural and inter-ethnic understanding and misunderstanding" (147).

So far as the writers of the Indian diaspora are concerned, from Raja Rao and G.V. Dasani to Jhumpa Lahiri and Arvind Adiga, a number of them have tried to give expression to their experiences and reflections. One can simply not miss out on Salman Rushdie, Vikram Seth, V.S. Naipaul, Bharati Mukherjee, Rohinton Mistry, M.G. Vassanji, Amitav Ghosh, Homi Bhabha, Gayatri Spivak, Firdaus Kanga, Boman Desai, Kiran Desai, Irwin Allen Sealy, Ardashir Vakil, Hari Kunzru, etc.

The area of diaspora studies is a **multidisciplinary** one which has linkages not only to literature but also to anthropology, geography, psychoanalysis, post-structuralist theory, history, cultural studies, etc. The postcolonial thinkers are involved in diaspora studies in a big way as the phenomenon of cross-continent migration picked up again after the decolonization. Among the leading **theorists** of the diaspora studies may be counted Edward Said, Homi Bhabha, Gloria Anzaldua, Stuart Hall, James Clifford, Paul Gilroy, Rey Chow, Arjun Appadurai, Theodor Adorno, Gilles Deleuze, Felix Guattari, etc.

The problem of identity is writ large all over diasporic literature. **Franz Fanon** (1925-61), the French-Algerian psychiatrist, in his book *Black Skin, White Masks* (1952) writes about the situation of the Antilles islands, which were the French colonies in the Caribbean and were populated mainly by the erstwhile black slaves brought there by the colonizer. Fanon comments that the language is the most significant identity marker and that its replacement with any other language—the colonizer's in this case—divests the colonized not only of his language but also of his cultural moorings. He notes that those black Antilleans in the French army, who had been taught French—the language of power—used other compatriots as interpreters to convey orders of their French masters to native Antilleans. Those Antilleans who understood French used French only to emphasize their difference from his compatriots. Most of the Caribbean people now speak Creole in place of their native language. A psychiatrist as he is, Fanon avers that this compulsive use of French impinges on the sense of identity of the native people—a black Diaspora—and affects their psyche.

Though the situation in India is a different one, **Homi K. Bhabha** (b. 1949) comments in Nation and Narration edited by him that "cultural difference emerges from the borderline moment of translation.... The transfer of meaning can never be total between differential systems of meaning" (314). In his book *Location of Culture* (2004), Bhabha expounds his concept of hybridity at length. The postcolonial discourse attaches great importance to the question of identity. First underlined in the context of newly-free nations, the notion was quickly taken up to describe the condition of any minority group pitted against a majority based on different colour, race, sex, etc. In the case of the immigrants in any society, their identity is threatened by the culture of the host country. The trajectory of a migrant follows the pattern of location, dislocation and relocation, each one of these phases being liminal rather than sharply defined ones. The process of acculturation is a slow one-sided (the minority seeking integration with the majority) one and is not without a sense of loss and exile. It is also not a clear transformation; it gives rise to hybridity marking different stages of acculturation. According to Homi Bhabha, "This interstitial passage between fixed identifications opens up the possibility of a cultural hybridity that entertains difference without an assumed or imposed hierarchy" (2004: 4).

In his *Decolonization and the Decolonized* (2006), **Albert Memmi** (b. 1920) reconsiders the myth of return with regard to the diaspora. The commonly held notion has been that the life of the migrant is temporary and sooner or later, he must return to his homeland after satisfying his quest for green bucks or career goals. But Memmi debunks this stand with regard both to literary characters and the discipline of ethnographic studies of the diaspora communities. The idea is that there is never a complete integration into the adopted society/country/culture. After spending time in the foreign country, the migrant will be at a loss to decide "which is here and which is there" (Ramone, 39).

Paul Gilroy (b. 1957), in his books *The Black Atlantic: Modernity and Double Consciousness* (1993) and *After Empire: Melancholia or Convivial Culture?* (2004) approaches the issue of diaspora through his concept of black Atlantic world. What he means by this is the interconnectednesss of all the black people living in the world on the basis of shared histories between the blacks and the whites. The latter point harks back to the times when the Europeans travelled to Africa, brought back Africans as slaves to work in the Caribbean and then shipped back to Africa the goods produced by those slaves. It does not merely lead to the feeling among the black people that they are both 'insiders' as well as 'outsiders' with regard to the West, but it also enables us to read the European history afresh. Gilroy considers "the culture of black Britain as something that develops alongside global black diaspora rather than as a discreet (sic) cultural entity within Britain" (Ramone, 119). What he means is that the development of Britain cannot be viewed as discrete or separate from the development of the black diaspora. Thus, the concept of relational identity of signifiers is transplanted in the area of racial development by him. On the other hand, W.E.B. DuBois, another theorist, argues that "'imprisonment' within racial identity meant that the racial group attained greater importance for the individual than the nation itself. Also segregation leads to inculcate a hatred of the other race" (Nayar, 273).

Works Cited

Ashcroft, Bill et al. *Key Concepts in Post-colonial Studies*. London: Routledge, Indian Reprint, 2004.

Bhabha, Homi K., ed. *Nation and Narration*. London: Routledge, 1990.

———. *The Location of Culture*. London: Routledge, 2004.

Hartley, John. *Key Concepts in Communication, Cultural and Media Studies*. London: Routledge, Third Edition, Indian Reprint, 2004.

Nandan, Satendra, "Diasporic Consciousness." *Interrogating Post-colonial Theory, Text and Context*. Ed. Harish Trivedi and Meenakshi Mukherjee. Shimla: Indian Institute of Advanced Studies, 1996.

Ramone, Jenni. *Postcolonial Theories*. New York: Palgrave Macmillan, 2011.

Rushdie, Salman. *Imaginary Homelands*. London: Granta Books, 1992.

Ryan, Michael. *Literary Theory: A Practical Introduction*. New York: Blackwell, 1999, Indian Reprint, 2002.

Sharma, J.C. Inaugural Address: "Indian Diaspora: Responsibilities and Relationships, Strengths, Weaknesses and Contribution." *Theorizing and Critiquing Indian Diaspora*. Ed. Adesh Pal. New Delhi: Creative, 2004.

23

Ecocriticism/Green Studies

Ecocriticism is the study of the relationship between literature and the physical environment. Both terms, 'ecocriticism' and 'green studies' are used to denote a critical approach which began in the USA in the late 1980s, and in the UK in the early 1990s. The signs of ecocriticism, as a literary concept, were first seen in America in the late 1970s, at the meetings of the Western Literature Association. Some critics trace its beginning to William Rueckerts' 1978 essay "Literature and Ecology: An Experiment in Ecocriticism". This critical field was earlier known as 'the study of nature writing'. But it was Cheryll Glotfelty, who initiated this critical approach as a lasting movement. In 1992, Glotfelty and Harold Fromm co-founded the Association for the Study of Literature and Environment. This organization has its own journal, called *ISLE* (*Inter-disciplinary Studies in Literature and Environment*). Both Glotfelty and Fromm co-edited a key collection of seminal essays—*The Ecocriticism Reade: Landmarks in Literary Ecology* (1996).

The movement in America took its inspiration from three major nineteenth-century American **transcendentalists**, namely Ralph Waldo Emerson (1803-18), Margaret Fuller (1810-50), and Henry David Thoreau (1817-62). They wrote about nature, life force, and the wilderness. All three were members of the informal group of New England writers, essayists and philosophers. They were known as transcendentalists. Emerson's long essay *Nature* was first published in 1836. In this essay, he talks about the impact of the natural world on him. Fuller's first book was *Summer on the Lakes, During 1843*. It is a powerful narrative of her encounter with the American landscape. Thoreau's *Walden* is an account of his two-year stay, from 1845, in a hut he had built on the shore of Walden Pond. It is the classic account of his attempt to renew the self through 'return to nature'. These three books can be seen as the foundational works of American 'eco-centred' writing. Apart from them, the mystic poet Walt Whitman is also known for his love of nature.

The UK version of ecocriticism better known as **Green Studies** takes its inspiration from the Romantic movement of late eighteenth century. However, its founding figure is the critic Jonathan Bate, author of *Romantic Ecology: Wordsworth and the Environmental Tradition* (1991). Raymond Williams' book *The Country and the City* (1973) is also taken by some as articulating ecological concerns, only the term 'ecocriticism' had not come into existence by that time. Ecocriticism, however, has not made as much progress as it has in the USA. Laurence Coupe's essay titled "The Green Studies Reader: From Romanticism to Ecocriticism" (2000) is taken as a seminal study.

Some of the debates within ecocriticism concern the crucial relationship between **nature and culture.** Ecocriticism rejects the major poststructuralist notion that everything is socially and/or linguistically constructed. For the ecocritic, nature exists in reality, whether or not it is textualised or part of the social discourse. According to Peter Barry, "it is out there, beyond ourselves, not needing to be ironised as a concept by enclosure within knowing inverted commas, but actually present as an entity which affects us, and which we can affect, perhaps fatally, if we mistreat it" (243). Barry explains it with an example related to topography. He refers to different manifestations of nature, as it is commonly understood, as expanses of green on uneven land. These are specified as,one, 'wilderness' that includes deserts, oceans and uninhabited continents; two, 'the scenic sublime' that is seen in the form of forests, lakes, mountains and waterfalls; three, 'the countryside' encompassing hills, fields and woods, and four, 'the domestic picturesque' as manifest in parks, gardens and lanes.

In these four 'areas', the 'pure nature' of wilderness is now being destroyed by the large-scale pollution let loose by human culture, thus pitting culture against nature. Moving from the first area to the fourth, we can mark the growing interference of culture in nature, so that the perfectly manicured lawns and gardens are supposed to be culturally perfect!

While the poets have always sung of nature, wild or urbanized, the **Marxist** school finds fault with the poets of 18th and 19th centuries like Thomas Gray and Wordsworth, for legitimizing inequality brought about by human culture as that produced by nature. Pictures of contented poor people in the lap of nature presented in poems like Thomas Gray's "Elegy written in a Country Churchyard" (1751), or Wordsworth's "The Prelude" (1805) are supposed to be tinged with bourgeois philosophy which dissuades working people from launching revolution for a better life. Thus, "Nature is the name under which we use the nonhuman to validate the human, to interpose a mediation able to make humanity more easy with itself" (Barry 244-45).

There has been a tradition in the West of treating nature as being there for the sake of man alone. This **anthropocentric** attitude is reflected in the Bible when God tells man to "fill the earth and subdue it; have dominion over the fish of the sea over the birds of the air, and over every living that moves on the earth" (Genesis 1: 28). Every herb and fruit growing on the earth was for man only. Before the Christian civilization began, the Greeks too believed similarly as is encapsulated in Protagoras's pronouncement, namely "Man is the measure of all things." The entire history of the Western civilization is full of endeavours to score victory over land, sea and air, and to tap natural resources wherever these are located. The result is there for us to see and suffer—polluted environment and even space, which bodes ill for the survival of mankind on this planet. In this science has been guilty of value-less advancement, as is suggested by William Howarth in his essay "Some Principles of Ecocriticism": "A source of both hope and fear, science presents solutions that only generate new problems, as in the bioethical riddles spawned by genetic engineering: should we destroy all 'defective' genes? To some critics, such questions suggest that scientists too often ignore the policy implications of their discoveries" (79).

Science, with all its paraphernalia to provide means of comfort to man has failed to provide a vision whereby man can co-exist with nature peacefully on the planet. It is left to 'nature writing' to waken man and to infuse in man the spirit of **symbiosis**. The notion of symbiosis opposes the Darwinian reading of nature in which might is right. There is no doubt that nature presents a world at once dark and bright. There is the Byronic mighty ocean that tosses about the ships and there is also the Wordsworthian nature that sends man into a meditative and peaceful mood. In this regard, Greg Gerrard's observation needs to be quoted: "Despite the obvious prevalence of predation in the natural world, it is hoped that, if we imagine symbiosis is more common than competition, we will be inspired to build more cooperative societies. The peaceful, mutually beneficial ecoexistence of algae and fungi in lichens, or mitochondria and cytoplasm in human cells, is no doubt, an example to us all" (8).

Some ecocritics vie with science and project literature also as a source of energy. Well-known ecocritic William Reuckert remarks:

> to discuss or read or study literature, is to gather energy centres around a matrix of sored poetic/verbal energy. In some ways, this is the true interactive field because the energy flow is not just a two-way flow from poem to person as it would be in reading; the flow is along many energy pathways from poem to person, from person to person. The process is triangulated, quadrangulated, multiangulated; and there is, ideally, a raising of the energy levels which makes it possible for the highest motives of literature to accomplish themselves. These motives are not pleasure and truth, but creativity and community. (110-11)

Ecocriticism, variously referred to as ecological, environmental or green criticism, then, can be summed up as follows:

1. It does not accept the social or linguistic constructedness of the world. The natural world exists in its own right and beings other than human have a will of their own. All beings have a right to habitat or home and congenial environment for their growth and survival.
2. It is a reading of a literary text which incorporates environmental concerns and issues. The ecocritics, in their attempt to bring environmental issues into focus, re-read major literary works and pay special attention to the representation of nature. In doing so, they go by concepts like growth, energy, balance and symbiosis.
3. The ecocritics also wish to find out what role has the physical-geographical setting played in the structure of a poem or a novel.
4. The ecocritics discuss factual details impacting environment like entropy or loss of energy on the one hand and sustainable sources of energy on the other. These are mostly found in essays, articles, travelogues, memoirs, etc.
5. The ecocritics have tried to create a separate canon highlighting authors who foreground nature in their subject matter. Some of these writers are the English Romantic poets, the American transcendentalists, the Georgian poets et al.
6. Finally, the ecocritics explore the link between academic and actual practices on the issue of nature.

Ecocriticism is the study of literature and environment from interdisciplinary point of view. At the same time, it may be pointed out that there is no single figure in the area of ecocriticism who can be considered as a dominant authority like Freud is in psychological criticism. All the sciences join together to analyze the environment and find out solutions for the contemporary environmental situation, e.g. global warming, etc. In comparison with other 'political' forms of criticism, there has relatively been little dispute about the moral and philosophical aims of eco-criticism and its scope has broadened rapidly. As such, 'nature-writing' or writing with consciousness of nature is emerging as a distinct and substantial genre and ecocriticism has already made its place as a literary theory.

Works Cited

Barry, Peter. *Beginning Theory: An Introduction to Literary and Cultural Theory*. Manchester, UK: Manchester University Press, 1999.

Gerrard, Greg. 'Ecocriticism and Consilience'. *Indian Journal of Ecocriticism*. OSLE India. Vol. 2, Aug. 2000.

Holy Bible. King James Version. Madras: India Bible Literature, 1980.

Howarth, William. 'Some Principles of Ecocriticism'. *The Ecocriticism Reader: Landmarks in Literary Ecology*. Eds. Cheryll Glotfelty and Harold Fromm. Athens and London: The University of Georgia Press, 1996, pp. 69-87.

Reuckert, William. 'Literature and Ecology'. *The Ecocriticism Reader: Landmarks in Literary Ecology*. Eds. Cheryll Glotfelty and Harold Fromm. Athens and London: The University of Georgia Press, 1996, pp. 105-23.

24

Stylistics

What started as a simple study of style of writing has grown into a rather unwieldy and complex field of stylistics now. It was perhaps, with this difficulty in mind that the French linguist Jean-Jacques Lecercle observed: "No one has ever known exactly what the term stylistics comprises yet the subject is forever being reborn" (Wales, 373). Simply put, the term 'style' refers to a certain mode of action or expression. Thus, a particular way of wearing clothes or of building a house, composing a piece of music or setting the dining table can be referred to as a particular style. In literature, by the term 'style', we normally understand the manner of writing—the way in which words are arranged to convey what the writer wishes to convey to the reader. This depends on a number of factors like diction, prosody, syntax, sound patterns, etc. The scope of style can be broadened to include imagery, metaphors, irony, foregrounding, etc.

Style is the **descendent of rhetoric** of yore. A rhetorician aimed at putting forth his views in a convincing manner so as to win over the court or the audience. For this, he depended upon rhetorical figures of speech or schemes which favoured using different patterns of words without bringing about any change in meaning like anaphora, zeugma, etc. These as well as the figures of thought or tropes like irony are therefore legitimate concerns of style. During Cicero's time, the principle of decorum decreed that the social class of the speaker and the occasion be kept in mind while deciding upon style. Over the period, based on different considerations, a number of classifications of style have emerged. Thus, we relate style to an individual, register, period, school, genre, etc. to form distinctions like Shakespearean, legal, Elizabethan, Romantic and poetic respectively. A long chain of scholars has contributed to the critical understanding of style and over the ages.

The **twentieth century** saw a lot of development that had a bearing on our understanding of style. The study of language took a turn with the appearance on the scene of the Swiss linguist Ferdinand de Saussure. He was responsible for putting the study of language on a scientific basis. Charles Bally, Saussure's pupil, who was the first to use the term 'Stylistics' in his book *Traite de stylistiquefrancaise* (1909), defined it as the "study of the 'affective' elements in language—these affective elements being conceived as optional additions to an already determinate meaning" (Hough, 6), which comes quite close to the Russian formalists' understanding of the subject. The Moscow group comprised linguists, literary critics and psychologists, who later developed the foregrounding theory. They opposed the Aristotelian mimetic theory and, in its place, favoured 'defamiliarisation' in literature because to them literature was just a linguistic product which had to be studied scientifically.

The Russian formalists were, in effect, the first stylisticians, but their work could not reach the Western academies because of the 1917 Bolshevik Revolution that transformed Russia into the Soviet Union. The gulf that emerged between the Western democracies and this newly-formed communist nation also impacted the academic domain. It was only in the 1960s, when Todorov translated some seminal texts into French that the West came to know of these tenets.

Roman Jakobson (1896-1982), a brilliant student of Moscow University, was a member of the **Moscow Linguistic Circle** and was associated with *avant-garde* art and poetry. He left Moscow in 1920, at the height of the Russian Revolution, and moved to Prague, to work on his doctoral thesis. Here, he became a member of the Prague Structuralist Circle. When

Czechoslovakia also became a communist country, Jakobson moved over to America in 1941, carrying along with him the seeds of what was to become stylistics later. The Prague group was also keenly interested in the linguistic structure of texts. Jan Mukarovsky, a member of this group, laid stress on the 'literariness' of text, i.e. the special use of language in a literary work which tended to 'foreground' the utterance. Victor Shklovsky, another formalist, termed this use of language as 'defamiliarizing' what was commonly observed but then this property was explained differently from the way the romantic critic Coleridge did. According to the revised notion, it is not the author who brings about defamiliarization, rather it is the language that performs the trick. Roman Jakobson identified these 'deviations' in phonological and grammatical constructions as also in versification and imagery.

The work of the Russian formalists belongs to the period of 1920s, but as mentioned earlier, due to the political turmoil engulfing the communist countries, the findings of the Russian formalists took time to reach the democratic society of the West. In the meantime, the critics I.A. Richards and William Empson had also been concentrating on the literary texts as also on the way readers were affected by those texts. This approach was called Practical Criticism—a term taken from Richards' book *Practical Criticism* (1929)—which gained ground in England of the 1930s. This approach, as also the literary essays of T.S. Eliot (*Selected Essays*, 1932), inspired a new movement in the U.S.A. called **New Criticism**—a term made popular by John Crowe Ransom's book *The New Criticism* (1941). Other advocates of this approach included Cleanth Brooks, René Wellek, R.P. Blackmur, Allen Tate and William K. Wimsatt. The new criticism was based almost exclusively on the close study of literary works as independent aesthetic objects, but practical criticism tended to pay more attention to the psychological aspects involved in the reader's interaction with the text. Later, the American new critics also focussed on features like irony, paradox and metaphor, but they did not apply the science of linguistics to poetry as the Russian formalists did.

Consequently, the traditional notion of style was replaced by what has come to be known as 'stylistics', meaning the science of style. It shows the growing impact of science which insisted on an objective study of literature. Some of the **early works** which laid down the roadmap for stylistics in Anglo-American criticism were Leo Spitzer's *Stilstudeien* (1928) and *Linguistics and Literary History* (1948), Thomas Sebeok's anthology titled *Style in Language* (1960), in which Roman Jakobson's article titled "Closing Statement: Linguistics and Poetics" appeared, Roger Fowler's edited work *Essays on Style in Language* (1966) and Geoffrey Leech's *A Linguistic Guide to English Poetry* (1969). The grammarian Bloomfield's article "Linguistic Aspects of Science" is also considered an important milestone in the importation of scientism in language study.

The increased interest in **scientific study** of language resulted in the evolution of linguistics to which the association of style gave rise to stylistics. In order to correct the bias in impressionistic analysis of texts, it undertakes the examination of lexis, grammar, syntax, phonological properties and discursive devices and leaves theme, character and environment of the text out. Stylistics has already re-defined some of the conventional **features**, as for example, alliteration, which is now called phonological parallelism. Apart from them, grammatical parallelism and deviation of language use from the normal one are considered foregrounding of language over literary features.

The increased focus on linguistic and stylistic categories pertaining to lexical, phonological and syntactical choices has the inherent danger of getting reduced to obsession with statistical data. In this regard, one cannot avoid mentioning Enkvist's formulation which is almost a **mathematical model.** He defines the linguistic aspect of stylistics as "the function of the aggregate of the ratios between the frequencies of its phonological, grammatical and lexical items and the frequencies of the corresponding items in a contextually related norm" (94). No wonder then that in their search for an out-and-out objective evaluation of literature, the stylisticians have also turned to computers to count different linguistic/grammatical elements. This method is called Stylometry.

This kind of stylistic examination, then, yields statistical figures that require **careful interpretation** even though some scholars believe that the meaning pre-exists in the language and it requires no further interpretation. According to Herbert Read, short sentences convey an impression of speed and therefore are suited to the description of action. Similarly, long sentences are indicative of deliberation and solemnity. The complex sentences suit complex ideas and feeling and anticipatory constituents in a sentence bring in an element of suspense. Fowler points out that tag questions are demanding and pointedly request confirmation of an assertion made already. Again, rhetorical questions, according to Quirk and Greenbaum, function as forceful statements, which of course, is nothing new since rhetoric has always been studied as the art of persuasive oratory.

Close reading for the sake of linguistic/stylistic analysis may be applied to a novel just as it is done in the case of a poem, but then one cannot hope to put the entire bulk of a novel through this mechanism. One could select at random one or more passages and submit them to close reading. There are limitations in applying this yardstick because "effective style analysis may or may not demand a rigorous stylistic or statistical examination. Such a thing might help in understanding a work that is linguistically complex; it may not be needed where the language follows normal conventions" (Batra, 2011: 17-18).

The **structuralists**, whose impact on style was enormous, based upon this twin-layered notion of sign, propounded mainly by Saussure. They viewed literature as an artifact of language. A poem was taken as a structure consisting of different units like words, sounds, punctuation, etc. The structuralist critics applied linguistic concepts to literary text, creating distinction between phonemic and morphemic levels of organization which meant the text was self-referential. The aim of the structuralist criticism was not to interpret individual texts, but to unveil the grammar embedded in a literary work which governed its form and meaning. Through the identification of this grammar, they hoped to underline how meaning is produced. The literary work was re-defined as a text whose author was declared dead by

Roland Barthes. The textuality, by extension, lost its distinction as purely literary outpouring and became "writing-in-general" (Abrams, 241).

The **poststructuralist phase** begins with Jacques Derrida, who gave the notion of deconstruction, and thereby changed the old fixity of meaning into an illusory trace—deferred and different forever and locked within the domain of language. However, Michel Foucault's notion of discourse changed the critical perspective again and brought milieu into the picture. Discourse connected text with context. So, stylistics now had two broad categories, as Bradford puts it: textualist and contextualist. Whereas the textualist stylisticians focus on prosody, metaphors, syntax, vocabulary, etc., the contextualists seek contexts in which reader's competence and socio-cultural forces affect systems of signification. Context is not mere physical circumstances but also the values, beliefs and ideas of the people living at a particular time in a particular society. Meaning and knowledge are no longer believed to pre-exist the text in the language itself. It may however be pointed out that the reader now has his subject position entirely as a product of social forces and practices. The literary phenomenon is viewed as a dialectic between such a reader and the text in which the meaning is generated.

The poststructuralist scenario, thus, is marked by **attention to semantics** alongside semiotics. It has been felt that the meanings derived from particular usage have become mechanistic and the context is being totally overlooked. Even the text, when it forms the immediate context of a passage selected for stylistic analysis, was relegated to background, disrupting the organic unity of the text. By underlining the importance of context, the overmuch stress on the linguistic aspect is sought to be balanced.

The concern with **socio-linguistic aspects** creates the stylistic genre called discourse analysis which has been in vogue since the 1970s. Discourse denotes all literary and non-literary verbal (spoken or written) construction or production in the linguistic mode. In this kind of analysis, language is taken as a living form that involves the speaker or writer addressing the hearer or the reader respectively. It also takes into account the situation and the socio-cultural conventions prevalent in a society at a particular point of time. It is based on the premise that both the speaker and the listener are aware of the linguistic code and the attendant connotational aspects so that the meaning becomes clear. "If an utterance seems purposely to violate these expectations, we seek to make sense of it by transferring it to a context in which it is clearly appropriate" (Abrams, 77).

This is a view that is opposed to that of the deconstructionists who viewed language as detached from history and discourse without a centre. In one respect, however, a section of the discourse analysts on the one hand and the deconstructionists on the other seem to agree and that is the belief that language alone cannot express what the writer wishes to convey through it. The reservation of the deconstructionists has already been mentioned; some discourse analysts feel that the surface meaning of a text is only a rouge used to cover what the writer could not say. Similarly, the gaps in a text are supposed to contain meaning.

The Foucauldian model of analysis called **Critical Discourse Analysis** takes into consideration the nature of discourse, which is defined as a set of relationships existing in society as a result of the power structure. This engagement of discourse with the power structure manifests itself in the form of rules, norms, social conventions and institutions. Incessant power struggle is a reality, according to Foucault, and it has a bearing on the existing structure and discursive formations.

This extension of stylistics has been justified as it seeks to find causal relationship between the stylistic character of literary texts and their social and ideological contexts. There seem minor differences between different approaches like those of the pragmatists, discourse analysts, socio-linguists, etc. but all of them are joined at the roots to culture. In addition to literature as we have known it, 'media-discourses' such as films, advertising, news reports, songs and political speeches have also been brought within the scope of stylistics. What is important to note here is that none of the text types gets precedence over any other.

Works Cited

Abrams, M.H. *A Handbook of Literary Terms*. New Delhi: Cengage Learning, 2009.

Batra, Jagdish. *Form and Style in Indian English Fiction*. New Delhi: Prestige, 2011.

Enkvist, N.E., Spencer et al. *Linguistics and Style*, Oxford University, 1964.

Hough, Graham. *Style and Stylistics*. New York: Routledge & Kegan Paul, 1969.

Read, Herbert. *English Prose Style*. Ludhiana: Lyall, 1968, p. 35.

Wales, Katie. *A Dictionary of Stylistics*. Essex: Pearson, 2001.

25

Narratology

Narratology, as the term indicates, is the study of a narrative, i.e. a story—in prose or verse. It could be a short story or a novel. In the case of poetry, a narrative poem can be subjected to narratological examination. Ancient literature in the form of epics or dramas thrived on narrative, although the manner of narration was different. Aristotle analyzed the ancient Greek drama and identified the beginning, middle and end of a play as worthy of attention by the dramatist. He also identified the elements of hamartia, peripeteia, anagnorisis, etc., which were and are even now considered vital to the development of character and action in the drama.

Since its origin in the eighteenth century, the novel has steadily risen in popularity. It occupies in contemporary times a position that can very well be compared to that of the drama in Elizabethan England. Narrative, being seminal to the novel, has therefore come to occupy a very important place and narratology, as the **science of narrative**, has expanded in scope and become an important subject of literary criticism now. The Russian formalists, followed by the French structuralists, have contributed a lot to the study of narratology. One encounters a plethora of terms linked to techniques or themes, as for example, structural narratology, cognitive narratology, visual narratology, natural narratology, confessional narratology, eco-narratology, feminist narratology, etc.

According to Jonathan Culler, narratology has many strands which are "implicitly united in the recognition that narrative theory requires a distinction between 'story', a sequence of actions or events, conceived as independent of their manifestation in discourse, and 'discourse,' the discursive presentation or narration of events" (189). Broadly speaking, the study of narratology can be divided into **two categories**—one that deals with the distinctions based upon the story, as for example, Vladimir Propp's analysis of folk tales. The other category pertains to the manner of telling the story and finding out elements like point of view.

Russian formalists like Viktor Shklovsky, Boris Tomashevsky, Tzvetan Todorov, etc. took up the study of narratives in which they identified strategies which had been used in plot construction. It was a new insight into literature that went a long way and developed the area of narratology. The central formalist distinction is between 'fabula' or story, which is the simple enumeration of chronological sequence of events, and '*suzhet*' or plot, which is how the narrative—myth or fictional work—uses the story. This distinction was first propounded by **Viktor Shklovsky** (1893-1984) in 1921. An author transforms the raw material of a story into a plot through the use of a variety of devices that violate sequence. While dealing with the basics of a fictional account, we realize that the actual story is amorphous and it has to be refined into a plot. Only then the reader will feel interested in it. The time in a plot could be stretched or amputated, depending upon the requirement of the story. It is virtually not possible to present on the stage or in the pages of a novel all that has happened in the life of different characters. We are interested in selective action that is relevant to the main interest or the theme of the text.

E.M. Forster points out in his *Aspects of the Novel* (1927), the basic difference between the two in this way: "While 'the king died and then the queen died' is a story, 'the king died and then the queen died of grief' is a plot. It means that the plot is based upon cause-effect relationship" (93). This is not to deny the role of probability in it because if it were always based upon causal nexus, there would be no 'defamiliarization' in it—a concept propounded by Shklovsky in his famous essay "Art as Technique" (1925). He underlined the importance of this concept mainly on the ground that the process of defamiliarization added to the aesthetic experience of the reader/viewer by prolonging it.

Another Russian formalist **Boris Tomashevsky** (1866-1939) distinguished between two kinds of arrangements: thematic elements that are ordered by causal temporal relationships from stories (narratives, tales, novels); and those that are contemporaneous. Working on narratology, he advanced the distinction between *fabula* and *suzhet*, which were first introduced by Shklovsky (Bertens, 36). Whereas fabula is the actual sequence of events as they happened, *suzhet* is the re-arrangement of details carried out to create literary effect. To the elements that advance the plot, he gave the name of *bound motifs*, while those which do not, he called *free motifs*.

In this respect, **Seymour Chatman's** five-fold division of time makes an interesting study: the *summary* abridges the time, while *ellipses* simply effaces time as in between the chapters or acts. Chunks of time—small or large—are normally dispensed with at such spots in a narrative. In scene, the story time and the narrative time are the same, but in stretch, the time is stretched so that the reader/viewer can absorb the intricacy of a situation. In the fifth category of pause, the story simply stops, as for example, when the author describes the scene or the objects and action takes a back-seat for a while.

Broadly speaking, the story/plot classification, as amended by the twentieth-century studies can be comprehended by the three-fold division based on 'story' (the actual order and timing of events), 'text' (the portrayal of events in the literary work) and 'narration' (the manner of telling). These three divisions are referred to as *historie*, *recit* and *narration* by another French narratologist **Gerard Genette** (b. 1930) who is indebted to the Russian formalists for the division.

Apart from the re-arrangement of events, the Russian formalists analyzed narratives to locate common thematic elements. In this area, **Vladimir Propp** (1895-1970) undertook a study of numerous Russian folklores and fairy tales in his

Morphology of the Folk Tale (1928, translated 1958), which became an epoch-making treatise. He zeroed in on seven actants or broad character-types and thirty-one basic 'functions' or areas of action. He classified characters into following groups: hero, false hero, villain, donor/provider, helper, princess and her father, and dispatcher. It is not necessary that in every narrative, all of them should be present, or that their functions should be exclusive. All tales proceed from a certain 'lack' or 'villainy'. Propp describes their roles beginning with the hero, who succeeds in getting the heroine after much struggle. The false hero is the one who tries to take credit for the actions of the hero so that he can marry the princess. The villain comes into the picture to oppose the hero. The donor or provider helps the hero, as for example, by giving him some magical wand. The helper can be a friend who helps the hero in his quest. The dispatcher makes the character realize the lack and sends him off.

Taking clues from the Russian formalists, the French anthropologist **Claude Levi-Strauss** (1908-2009) took up a number of myths and found that in thousands of them, the narratives contained some basic thematic structures. His notion of **mythemes** is modelled upon Saussure's phonemes. What he discovered was that like the self-referentiality of the linguistic signs, the myths seemed to relate to one another, rather than to reality. **A.J. Greimas** (1917-92) reduced this pattern further to certain binaries which included six actants or roles. These were—subject/object to account for the basic patterns of desire, aim or search; sender/receiver for conveying messages, etc., and helper/opponent for auxiliary actions.

Another French scholar **Roland Barthes'** (1915-80) classification of *catalytic/indexical*, corresponding to Chatman's *kernels/satellites* categories, refers to the events contributing to the furtherance of the narrative and the attending details like scenic or atmospheric description respectively. Instead of the inductive method of studying various narratives and then laying down the common points as Propp had done, Roland Barthes used the deductive method by breaking up Balzac's *Sarassine* into 561 segments in his book *S/Z*. He brought in linguistic elements and exploited their semantic worth to analyse a narrative just as he would a sentence, but such an approach, called *explication de texte*, providing for a long commentary—much more elaborate than the target text—could find few followers (Sturrock, 118).

Regarding the **'telling' aspect** of the story, we find that Boris Eichenbaum (1886-1959), another leader of the Russian formalist group, dealt with this aspect in his famous essay on Gogol's story "Overcoat", in which he analyzed the story without reference to extra-literary referents. He expressed the view that it was the 'telling' of the story or skaz, as he called it, which produced a grotesque effect on the reader by dishing out irrelevant detail and shifting the tone suddenly from comic to pathetic. Thus, the manner and tone of description play an important role in a narrative.

As with the narrative, **the narrator** has also been classified by Gerard Genette into categories like *autodiegetic*, in which the narrator as the main protagonist relates the story in the first person, as in Aravind Adiga's novel *The White Tiger* in which Ashok, the chauffeur, relates his own life story; *homodiegetic* in which the character in the narrative is not the leading one and is mainly used to report the events as in the case of Mr. Lockwood or Mrs. Dean in Emily Bronte's novel *Wuthering Heights*; and *heterodiegetic* in which the narrator is the omniscient author who is outside the narrative and tells the story in the third person, as is the norm in most traditional novels. In contemporary novels, it is not uncommon to find a mélange of different types of narration in one text.

Talking about **narrative style**, it may be noted that it is not necessary for the plot to proceed in a linear fashion. A narrative can begin in *media res*, or in the middle and reveal the beginning later at an appropriate spot. As an example, we can refer to Shakespeare's play *Hamlet*, which begins with the dialogue between two guards about the appearance of the murdered king's ghost. The real amorphous story began with the infatuation of Claudius for Gertrude which was the reason for the murder of old king Hamlet. In most movies, the device of flashback or *analepses* is used. Most of the murder stories begin from a point where the crime has been committed and then there is a journey back in time to reveal the background. At times, the writer may jump to future and hint at what is to come. While concluding her novel *The Namesake*, Jhumpa Lahiri tries this trick and tells about what the protagonist Gogol's mother would do but the novel ends soon thereafter, without letting the mother accomplish what was revealed by the author. This device is called *propleses*.

Apart from this, the **point of view** becomes an important issue in the narrative. It is the attitude of the narrator towards the events. This can sway the reader's sympathies because the narrator is also the interpreter. Thus, the world is seen through children's eyes in Arundhati Roy's *The God of Small Things* and it is the children's point of view through which the reader is informed of events. Also the plot of the novel takes its flight from the present when the twins Estha and Rahel are 31-year old but soon the narration focalizes at the stage when they were children. The children have grown up but for the purpose of telling the story, they revert to childhood. Such a strategy is also called focalization.

The **narrative mode** also has various types; it can be direct, indirect, or Free Indirect Discourse. According to Leech and Short, when the spoken words in a text are quoted without any reporting verb, the writing is referred to as Free Direct Speech, as for example: *He said I'll come back here to see you again tomorrow*. The same idea can be put in a different form which is called Free Indirect Speech. The sentence quoted before will now become: *He would return there to see her again the following day* (325). This style, also called F.I.D. (Free Indirect Discourse) by Shlomith Rimmon-Kenan, is used for interior monologue. Both these forms are freely used in fiction these days.

Closely allied to this mode is the technique of **Stream-of-Consciousness**. The term has been in vogue since the 1920s, when the psychologist William James used it to describe the unbroken flow of conscious and unconscious thoughts, feelings, perceptions, memories, etc. While the writer's rendering of the thought processes of characters bears the tell-tale signs of the author's hand in Stream-of-Consciousness, the Interior

Monologue is free from it. In his sincere effort to portray the goings-on in the human mind, the author has been faulted for dressing up in language the perceptions, thoughts, feelings, etc. which may have existed at the pre-language level. In his unique work, *The Life and Opinions of Tristram Shandy, Gentlemen*, the eighteenth-century pioneer of the genre of novel, Lawrence Sterne, had resolved this point by presenting in the pages of his novel, paintings or dots and dashes or simply leaving the pages blank to represent various states of mind including vacuity. However, in contemporary fiction, the writers prefer to convert the non-verbal segments into verbal ones.

Narratology began basically as a formalist/structuralist enterprise. It was not supposed to help in exploring the relationship between the text and the author or between the text and the social context. In these postmodern times, newer concepts continue to turn heads. Theoreticians like Roland Barthes, Claude Bremond and Francois Lyotard have freed narrative from fiction and even literature. "No sooner had narrative come of age as a theoretical concept than it began to invade fields as diverse as historiography, medicine, law, psycho-analysis, and ethnography" (Ryan, 344). Therefore, "the term 'narrative of the science' is as acceptable to postmodern critic as the 'narrative of history'. At the root of this chaos lies the feeling that what was known as reality to our ancestors is now a 'narrative', a fictitious one at that, which would not exclude even science" (Batra, 27).

Works Cited

Batra, Jagdish. *Form and Style in Indian English Fiction*. New Delhi: Prestige, 2011.

Bertens, Hans. *Literary Theory: The Basics*. Oxford: Routledge, 2001.

Culler, Jonathan. *The Pursuit of Signs: Semiotics, Literature, Deconstruction*. London: Routledge, 2001.

Forster, E.M. *Aspects of the Novel*. Harmondsworth, U.K.: Penguin, 1962.

Rimmon-Kenan, Shlomith. *Narrative Fiction*. London: Routledge, 1983, edition 2005.

Leech, Geoffrey N. and Michael H. Short. *Style in Fiction*. London: Longman, 1981, Fourth Reprint, 1985.

Ryan, Michael. *Literary Theory: A Practical Introduction*. New York: Blackwell, 1999, Indian Reprint, 2002.

Sturrock, John. *Structuralism*. (Second edition). Oxford, UK: Blackwell, 2003.

26

Intertextuality

The concept of intertextuality developed in France in the 1960s. "Intertextuality" according to Ross Murfin and Supriya M. Ray, is "the condition of interconnectedness among texts, is the concept that any text is an amalgam of others" (219). In the context of a given text, it refers to the signs of influence of other texts in some form or the other. It could be through literary devices like as allusions, quotations, genre, style, etc. Intertextuality has now become increasingly significant as a way of thinking about how a literary text is produced and comes to acquire meaning. The critic Julia Kristeva, who popularized and is often credited with coining this term in the 1960s, views any given work as part of a large fabric of literary discourse.

That the intertextuality has always been practised, though seldom recognized as such, is borne out by the comments of great writers like Thomas Hardy who recognized this kind of process when he said, "Each new style of novel must be the old with added ideas, not an ignoring and avoidance of the old" (qtd. Sermon, 233). Hardy's fiction is of course very repetitive in several respects. A metaphor which Hardy uses in various contexts is of a '**palimpsest**', which is a term for a manuscript page from a scroll or book from which the text has been scraped or washed off and which can be used again to write something upon. The term has been dealt with in the context of intertextuality by Gerard Genette.

One of the most influential critics of the twentieth century has been **Mikhail Bakhtin** (1895-1975), a Russian literary critic and theoretician. His concept of *heteroglossia* can be taken as the starting point of the notion of intertextuality. Bakhtin believed that a novel is a dialogic amalgam of different voices, by which he meant that it referred to different discourses, as for example, those of history, literature, sociology, philosophy, etc. Also, when different characters express their various viewpoints, they show their existence independently of the author and therefore, the novel is not just the voice of the novelist. It is clear that Julila Kristeva propounded the concept of intertextuality on the basis of Bakhtin's theory.

In *The Bounded Text* (1980), **Julia Kristeva** (b. 1941) establishes the manner in which a text is constructed out of already existing discourse. Authors do not create their texts from their own minds, but rather compile them from pre-extant texts. In her *Desire in Language* (1980), Kristeva defines the text as "'a permutation' of texts, an intertextuality: in the space of a given text, several utterances, taken from other texts, intersect and neutralize one another". Other critics have argued for an even broader use and understanding of the term intertextuality. They maintain that literary history, by itself, is too narrow a context within which to understand a literary text.

Structuralist critic **Gerard Genette** (b. 1930), in his books *The Architext: An Introduction* (1979), *Palimpsests: Literature in the Second Degree* (1982) and *Paratexts: Thresholds of Interpretation* (1987), has formulated a comprehensive typology of various relationships among texts. Under the umbrella term of *transtextuality*, loosely defined as "everything that sets it into secret or overt relation to othertexts, Genette differentiates five major types of relationship between texts" (Onega, 277). These are: *architextuality, intertextuality, paratextuality, hypertextuality,* and *metatextuality*. While *architextuality* determines the generic nature of a given text, the concept of intertextuality is expanded to include in it not only its relation to other texts, but to other portions of the same text also. Besides, it refers to the references, allusions, citations and even plagiarized sections of other texts. Similarly, *paratextuality* establishes the relationship between texts and the epigraphs, prefaces, forwards, acknowledgements, footnotes, illustrations, etc. which are included in a given literary text. *Hypertextuality* studies the relationship between a text, called 'hypertext' here and a preceding one, called 'hypotext'. Thus, the relationship between James Joyce's *Ulysses* and Homer's *Odyssey* is that of 'hypertext' to 'hypotext'. Again, metatextuality is the relationship of critical commentaries of a text and the text itself.

The **post-structuralist** critics do not regard the writer as a great originator or a creative genius; rather they view the author as a synthesizer—someone who draws together and organizes linguistic raw materials. In this sense, literature becomes a form of repetition to some extent. For example, myths keep recurring in modified forms. The Oedipus story would indicate this because its variants keep appearing in literary history. Shakespeare's *Hamlet* too, has affinity with this story. The repeated use of the Grail or the Quest motifs in chivalric tales and Arthurian legends has been repeated, with some variations, in texts like Joseph Conrad's novel *Heart of Darkness* and T.S. Eliot's long poem "The Waste Land". All these examples show how a particular story or myth can be repeated in different ways.

The point of view may change in such revisions but that too does not take away from the revised text the element of intertextuality. More specific instances would be the way in which Charlotte Bronte's famous novel *Jane Eyre* has clearly been reworked in Daphne Dumaurier's *Rebecca* (1936). It is also re-written from the point of view of Mrs. Rochester in Jean Rhys's Wide *Sargasso Sea* (1966). John Fowles' *The French Lieutenant's Woman* (1969) contains many quotations from historical, sociological, biological, geographical and literary texts which are woven into the narrative. It has also indirect allusions to nineteenth and twentieth century conventions. *A Thousand Acres* (1991) by Jane Smiley is a re-telling of Shakespeare's *King Lear*, against the backdrop of rural Iowa is another famous example of intertextuality.

Roland Barthes (1915-80), in his story, "Theory of the Text", remarks, "Any text is a new tissue of past citations" This view of the text as a *network* helps partly to explain what is meant by the term, i.e. a text consists of multiple writings which are drawn from a range of discourses, already in circulation in one form or the other. Literary textuality then can be seen as a kind of discursive recycling. But the new relations which come to exist between the discourses appropriated and incorporated into a text ensure that literary writing is never the same, never completely repeated.

Michel Foucault (1926-84) in his book *The Archaeology of Knowledge* expresses the opinion that "The frontiers of a book are never clear-cut: beyond the title, the first line and the last full stop...it is caught up in a system of references to other books, other texts, other sentences..." (23). A text is constantly rewritten into a variety of different material, social, institutional and ideological contexts. In a sense, all texts undergo a process of rewriting as they are re-read and reproduced.

Intertextuality, as a term, has not been restricted to discussions of the literary arts only. It is also applied to **other art forms** like cinema, painting, music, architecture, photography—almost all cultural and artistic productions. In spite of the commonsense association between literature and 'text', it is possible to speak of the 'languages' of cinema, painting or architecture. Other critics see intertextual features in painting and photography also. Intertextuality can be seen as connected to a developing trend within twentieth century art to incorporate 'real objects' into painting. Thus we can say that intertextuality, as a term, is not confined to literature alone but it embraces other disciplines also. The importance of the World Wide Web is too manifest to be underlined here. It has also been theorized as a unique realm of reciprocal intertextuality, in which no particular text can claim centrality.

Many critics welcome the fact that intertextuality as a term is available and argue for its positive advantage over more established terms in their fields. But some critics have complained that the ubiquity of the term "intertextuality" in postmodern criticism has crowded out related terms and important nuances. They also lament that intertextuality has overshadowed allusion as an object of literary study. Linda Hutcheon argues that excessive interest in intertextuality and rejects the role of the author, because intertextuality can be found "in the eye of the beholder" and does not entail a communicator's intentions. By contrast, in *A Theory of Parody*, Hutcheon notes parody always features an author who actively encodes a text as an imitation with critical difference.

A pertinent objection could be in the form of charge of plagiarism against intertextuality. As Onega states it, "Genette himself acknowledges it is often difficult in practice to separate some categories from others. For instance, the difference between plagiarism (a form of intertextuality) and imitation (a form of hypertextuality) or between citation (a form of intertextuality) and pastiche (a form of hypertextuality) often depends exclusively on the intenteionality that the reader attributes to the author" (277).

Works Cited

Foucault, Michel. *The Archeology of Knowledge*. New York: Pantheon Books, 1972.

Hutcheon, Linda. *A Theory of Parody: The Teachings of Twentieth-Century Art Forms*. New York: Methuen, 1985.

Onega, Susana. "Structuralism and Narrative Poetics", *Literary Theory and Criticism*. Ed. Patricia Waugh. Oxford: Oxford University Press, 2006, Third Impression, 2009, pp. 259-79.

Mitra, Ananda. "Characteristics of the wwwText: Tracing Discursive Strategies". *Journal of Computer-Mediated Communication* 1999: 5 (1): 1.

Murfin, Ross and Supriya M. Ray. *The Bedford Glossary of Critical and Literary Terms*, Second Edition. New York: St. Martin's, 2003.

Sermon, G.W. *The Pessimism of Thomas Hardy*. Fairleigh: Dickinson University Press, 1976.

27

Film Studies

Film studies, sometimes taken to be part of the media studies, is an academic discipline that deals with various theoretical, historical and critical approaches to films. It also takes up the study of psychology of audience and broader issues of socio-cultural, economic and ideological importance. There is no gainsaying that the genre of film studies is a new one as compared to literary studies. Literary pundits had always had an upper hand in critiquing films but later of course the realization gained ground that literature and cinema were two distinct categories of expression and films required a different approach than the one for literature. No doubt, narrative forms the backbone of both genres but then the films require much more than the written word that signifies concepts and experience. It also banks largely upon the physical apparatus like camera, sound recording equipment, light reflectors, etc. A plunge into the history of the visual media is necessary to appreciate the evolution of the critical canon in films.

The Lumiere brothers showed their first film, called *Actualties* at that time in 1895 in Paris. It was only around the time structuralism appeared on the scene that the film theory and criticism also made its appearance felt. In 1919, the Moscow Film School was inaugurated which was the first school in the world that focused on the then new area of films. It is now renamed as All Russian University of Cinematography. A decade later, the first institute for the study of filmic art—USC School of Cinematic Arts was established in America.

To begin with, film criticism was largely descriptive, though at times it tended to be judgmental also. Among the **early theoreticians**, the credit for being the pioneer in this field goes to the French critic Riccioto Canudo, the writer of *The Birth of the Seventh Art* (1911). It was followed by the poet Vachel Lindsay's *Art of the Moving Picture* (1915) and the psychologist Hugo Munsterberg's *The Photoplay: A Psychological Study* (1916). Lindsay sought to make a comparative study of the film vis-à-vis other art forms like poetry and architecture. Munsterberg, however, focused on the unique properties of cinema as also on the psychological responses of the viewers. His viewpoint was significant because "In relating the world depicted on the screen to the actual world and in demonstrating film's capacity to reformulate time and space to create the mental process of the imagination, Munsterberg was implicitly introducing a critical issue that would be the focus of much of the theoretical discussion of cinema for the next 40 years, namely, the tension between realism and formalism" (Konigsberg, 343).

Much of the early film criticism of the first half of the twentieth century is known as the **classical formalist** film theory. It was formalistin outlook and it distinguished films as a genre from other art forms. Besides, it focussed on camera work and cinematic codes. It was suited to the silent films of these times. A name that hogged the limelight in film studies circles was that of the impressionist critic Louis Delluc, whose first collection of articles was published in 1919. His compilation Photogenie (1920), by sheer choice of the term, highlighted the capacity of cinema to present real world afresh, besides helping the viewers to comprehend the beauty of the world. Lev Kuleshov, a Russian film-maker, outlined the theory of montage. He underlined convincingly that juxtaposition of individual shots created a unique emotional impact and also a meaning which was not available in the shots singly. It was left to Kuleshov's pupil V.I. Pudovkin to come up with the idea of filmic space and time which were different from the real space and time. Eisenstein propounded his theory of 'collision' in montage and articulated forcefully that juxtaposition of shots could create a single perception that transcended the realistic imagery.

The change to the **classical realist phase** was linked to the shift from the silent films to what we in India call 'talkies', films with natural and artificial sound effects. It was indeed a revolutionary shift and it lasted till the 1960s. The silent films could not claim to be realistic because they lacked sound which is an integral feature of the real world. The background music incorporated in the silent movies also did not match the external reality. However, the change also raised hackles of some critics who had developed a love for the images and found it to be the real art. The American film directors Orson Welles and William Wyler made use of deep focus and long shots which represented the external reality in a better way. Walter Benjamin's famous essay "The Work of Art in the Age of Mechanical Reproduction" (1932) argued that the 'aura' or the uniqueness of the living being could not be replicated in films because these were mechanical productions. Rudolph Arnheim, who was one of the principal practitioners of the formalist film school argued that films did not simply copy the reality but also interpreted and moulded it.

Content became more important than the form in the classical realist mode of film criticism. Andre Bazin, the founder of the French film journal *Cahiers du cineme*, founded in 1951, had great influence on the films of his time. Another noted theorist of the classical realist school was Siegfried Kracauer. Their film theory depended to a great extent on theory of literary realism and naturalism which held sway in the 19th and early 20th centuries. It was believed that the medium of films could accurately represent historical and social reality. To achieve this, it was necessary to absorb the reader in the film and provide to him the maximum detail through 'deep focus', somewhat like the realist novels of Thomas Hardy or Charles Dickens which captured minute details of the environment. In the context of films, transitions of shots were effected in a natural and unobtrusive manner. Kracauer's theoretical work Theory of Film: *The Redemption of Physical Reality* (1960) stresses the importance of letting the viewer connect to the world that he has been accustomed to seeing around him, which means the filmic narrative should not distort reality. Jean Mitty, in his two-volume work *Esthetique etpsychologie du cinema* (1963-65) tries to reconcile the realist and formalist viewpoints by arguing that filmic images are replicas of the objects and people around us but the filmic art imposes on these significance and meaning.

An important formulation which came to stay for a long time was the Auteur theory. Francois Truffaut in his essay "A Certain Tendency in French Cinema" (1954) advanced this theory, which became very popular with Andrew Sarris taking it up in his essay "Notes on the Auteur Theory in 1962". Like the author of a book (in fact, 'auteur' in French means the author), the director of a film too is the most important person in the making of a film. His vision and style make or mar the film. Thus, literature and film were put at par with each other. Drawing inspiration from literature, another theory that achieved prominence around the same time was the Genre theory. It focused on the commonalities in different films and studied the linkage between films and audiences. Hollywood was producing a large number of films and such a pattern of study suited the course of criticism.

The decade of 1960s is known for the revolutionary fervor which gripped much of Europe, which showed a pronounced leftist inclination. A record number of 32 African nations won their independence. France saw widespread student unrest in 1968. Rise of counter-culture took place in many societies, which showed in clothing, music, education, etc. Social taboos with regard to sex and race mellowed down. Anti-war and anti-racism demonstrations took place in America. Feminism and gay rights movements were also very effective. All this provided much grist to the cinema mill and the politicization of cinema seemed imminent.

However, it was also the period when film theory became an academic discipline. In literature and philosophy, **structuralism** was in ascendance during the period of 1960s and 1970s. Cinema resonated to the academic revolution that was influenced by the theory of signification propounded by Saussure. According to Konigsberg,

> The binary oppositions and structures explored in these studies may seem too superficial to suggest the deep structures that Clause Levi Strauss had propounded in myths from 'primitive' cultures in his treatment of the Oedipus myth but a work such as Jim Kitses' *Horizons West* (1969) is able to establish a basic structural and thematic dialectic in the Western and also to show the individual contributions of specific directors within this context. (344)

The lead in incorporating structuralism into film studies was given by Christian Metz, who developed a kind of film semiotics in his *Film Language: A Semiotics of Cinema*, first published in French in 1968 and translated into English in 1974. He was also obliged to the American philosopher C.S. Peirce, the Marxist scholar Althusser, the French psychologists Sigmund Freud and Jacques Lacan. He believed that meaning could be obtained through semiotic codes which he organized into 'grandesyntagmatique'. Metz divided the filmic narrative into eight 'syntagmas' or independent shots. Although poststructuralism dented structuralism to some extent, yet the structuralist study of films has not totally abated.

Many critics like Stephen Heath, Colin MacCabe and Peter Wollen disfavoured the structuralist theory and the concept of binary oppositions in understanding the film. They supported the view that cinema had a role to play in the revolutionary change in society. The structuralist-formalist moves were dubbed as "ultimately satisfactory foray into a rigorous application of semiotics to cinema" (Milliken, 349). Many scholars felt these overlooked the drastic political events of 1968 which necessitated response from the cinema. In these circumstances, the ideas of the Frankfurt School which was based upon neo-Marxist interdisciplinary approach carried great appeal. The school was known for its derisive reference to the media as 'culture industry' and its advocacy of social slant to art and literature. Theodor Adorno, an important member of the school, was not appreciative of the fantasy world projected by the cinema as it discouraged independent thinking. In England, the followers of F.R. Leavis led a frontal attack on the so-called vulgar mass culture. Film theory had veered round to the view that films were political in nature. Films were evaluated on the basis of their ability to support or condemn the prevailing social ideology.

The **rise of feminism** in the 1970s also contributed to concern for women in the cinema. The plight of women as also their representation in the visual media became a point of attention. *Camera Obscura* was among the first few women's journals. The decade of 1980s saw the escalation of interest in the psychoanalytical theories of Freud and Lacan. Laura Mulvey's essay "Visual Pleasure and Narrative Cinema" (1975) focused on the 'male gaze' and spawned a number of writings based on what was called 'the language of desire'. According to her, the cinema depicts women from the male point of view. It puts the audience in a masculine subject position and the woman on the screen is seen as an object of desire. Further, Mulvey also distinguishes between two types of male gaze: voyeuristic and fetishistic. While the first looks upon the woman as no better than a prostitute, the latter sees her as a sublime Madonna or Virgin Mary who cannot be appropriated.

Woman is portrayed as the passive object of male desire but the "pleasure of the male gaze is threatened by the woman's representation as a signifier of castration" (Konigsberg, 345). This theory has been criticized for not being based upon empirical evidence. Mulvey also made use of the Lacanian 'mirror theory' in which the child after looking at his image for the first time, understands that it is how it looks and how it may look better for the other's gaze. She extends this idea suggesting that the silver screen looks like a metaphorical mirror which reflects back to the female viewer representations of female identity although these are not the genuine reflections of the viewer, yet rather the male perceptions of idealized femininity. The female viewer is attracted to it in a bid to look better for the male gaze. Other feminist film theorists are Gaylyn Studlar, Kaja Silverman, etc. As in the case of feminist studies in literature, the concern for masculinity and homosexuality has crept into film studies over the years.

Another potent development of the 1970s was the impact of Lacanian **psychology** on the Hollywood. Keeping pace with this development, the famous critic Metz became a convert to the psychological criticism as evidenced in his book *The Imaginary Signifier* (1977, trans. 1982). He "attempted to create metapsychology of the cinema, arguing that film mobilizes techniques of the imaginary and engages processes of the unconscious more than does any other artistic, medium" (Milliken, 349). Other aspects of film like sound and music are also studied. Besides, issues of race too were subsumed under the psychological umbrella even though these rightly belong to the area of postcolonial studies.

These developments and diversions are what constitutes **postmodern pluralism**, most prominent in the post-1970 period. Films have been made on a large number of themes and experiments have been conducted in filmic style as well. A clear poststructural trait to be found is the severance of link between the author and the style here. There are multiple styles in a single film that create a polyphony of voices. Films have been a part of the popular culture. As such, popular themes ranging from murder mysteries, horror films, science fiction and romances to those touching on historical, political and social themes are quite common. At the same time, there is least regard for historical truth. In the postmodern film, the characters represent the postmodern ethos, as described by Jean Lyotard: "one listens to reggae, watches a western, eats McDonald's food for lunch and local cuisine for dinner, wears Paris perfume in Tokyo and 'retro' clothes in Hong Kong" (Answering).

Contemporary film criticism is an extension of the mood set in that decade. But it is also a reaction to the psychological and Marxian approaches. Greater stress is now laid on the form and technique and the examination of viewer's responses. In all these, the literary theoretical concepts guide the genre of film studies. The cinematic history has been examined afresh as for example, in celebrated philosopher Giles Deleuze's *Cinema I: the Movement-Image* (1986) and *Cinema 2: The Time-Image* (1986). The domain of cultural studies has come to have a broader engagement with film studies. The digital revolution has added to the appeal of the visual media but it has also projected the unreal or the 'hyperreal' as the only real.

Naturally, the area of film studies is now full of a mélange of postmodern approaches in their newer versions, as for example, poststructuralist semiotics and neo-formalism. Film studies is now focused on the narratological, artistic, cultural, economic and political aspects of the cinema. On the whole, film studies has been "conducted from a rich variety of perspectives, including culture, authorship, genre, the study of film stars, Marxism, psychoanalysis, feminism, and ethnicity" (Habib, 195). However, it would be appropriate to remind ourselves of what the postmodern philosophers like Fredric Jameson observe about films. He finds that the postmodern films are governed by a nostalgia—"an alarming and pathological symptom of a society that has become incapable of dealing with time and history" (qtd. Woods, 212). Hence, we revel in the celebration of the signifier alone, i.e. the present only.

Works Cited

Habib, M.A.R. *Modern Literary Criticism and Theory: A History*. Oxford: Blackwell, 2008, Reprint, 2013.

Konigsberg, Ira. "Film Theory and Criticism: Classic Topics and Later Developments: Classic Topics and Later Developments". *John Hopkins Guide to Literary Theory & Criticism*. Second Edition. Eds. Groden, Michael et al. Baltimore: The John Hopkins University Press, 2005.

———. "Answering the question: what is the postmodern?" Talk by Jean-Francois Lyotard. Sydney, Power Publications, 1992. 9 August 2013
http://www.marginalutility.org/wp-content/uploads/2010/04/machete_reading_may1_c.pdf

Milliken, Christie. "Film Theory and Criticism: Classic Topics and Later Developments: May 1968 and Beyond". *John Hopkins Guide to Literary Theory & Criticism*. Second Edition. Eds. Groden, Michael et al. Baltimore: The John Hopkins University Press, 2005.

Woods, Tim. *Beginning Postmodernism*. New York: Manchester University Press, 1999.

28

Televisual and Cyberspace Studies

With the unprecedented growth of media in our times, the area of media studies is also getting enriched. The term 'medium' whose plural form is 'media', refers to any material through which something else maybe transmitted. An artist uses the paint to convey his message whereas an author uses pen to transmit his ideas. Media of communication are any means by which messages are transmitted, but in common usage, the term refers to mass media. The media are therefore, can be described as "the content industries devoted to reaching very large popular audiences and readerships in print (newspapers, magazines, popular publishing), screen (cinema, TV) and aural (recorded music, radio) media" (Hartley, 142). These media impact popular culture to a great extent and therefore, are of interest not only to the discipline of cultural studies, but also to psychology, anthropology, sociology, etc.

Now, newspapers, magazines and journals have been around since the 18th century and music has been in this world since times immemorial, the development of visual media is a singular feature of **recent historical development**. Since the 1970s, the television has progressed tremendously and has now entered almost every home, following in the footsteps of radio, but beating the latter as a moulder of culture because the visual has more impact than the aural. Another important development of our times is the computer-aided virtual world or cyberspace. The Internet connectivity has at once brought the world together, obliterating distance and time. People can now exchange information and ideas, conduct business, provide social and political support, play games, and do a myriad other things. This is bound to influence culture of contemporary times. In this section, therefore, we shall focus on the two entities—the television and the internet, both joined through the technology of the televisual or the ability to view images along with the sound over a distance—long or short.

Taking up the functioning and impact of the television in contemporary world, it is generally believed that **the news** telecast is true and accurate. Without going into the issue of fallibility of knowledge as pointed out by the new historicists, and believing that those responsible for broadcasting the news intend giving the right information to the viewers, it is still a matter of pick and choose for the news desk editor. Out of the plethora of news pouring in at any given point of time, the news editor is to decide which news to include in the evening bulletin and which to exclude, the order and importance to be given to each news and more than that from which angle to broadcast it. The subjectivity of the editor is a product of the prevailing discourse. The power structure, we know, controls the discourse in the final analysis. As such, the news is also not above board.

The **postmodern distinctions** in the functioning of television are many. It is accused of being responsible for the decline of reason in society. The narrative is no longer important, nor is authority respected. The postmodern television exhibits traits like frequent intertextuality and even plagiarism, abrupt transitions, pastiche, linguistic and visual puns, fragments, etc. Reflexivity in the form of movie about movie-making is a trend just as the distinction between the stage and the audience has vanished. Thus, the medium has become more important than the message and style has upstaged content. Similar postmodern traits can be found in contemporary music also. According to Peter Wollen, "The polarized distinction between avant-garde and kitsch, high and low art; the doctrine of the purity of genres; the cluster of aesthetic concepts around the idea of artistic originality—all these are useless for any serious engagement with a hybrid and technologically sophisticated form such as music video" (Woods, 205).

John Fiske, author of the celebrated work *Television Culture* (1987), supports this premise of 'transparency fallacy' through his intention to "study the ways by which television produces 'reality' rather than reflect it" (21). News room has its own conventions by which it struggles to bring different news under its format and thus controls the dissemination of news. There are two axes of paradigmatic and syntagmatic selection followed. The paradigmatic axis comprises selection and categorization, whereas the syntagmatic axis has the processes of combination and narrativization. Fiske quotes some critics to suggest that "for an event to be deemed newsworthy, it should be recent, concern elite persons, be negative, and be surprising" (282). So, it is not really the concern to present truth and only the truth but some different consideration.

Another insight provided by Fiske is that the television programmes serve the ends of socially dominant ideology. All this leads one to the

> general belief, even among the most optimistic of liberals, that real news is too often image manipulation, that the dissemination of basic information is always distorted by business corporate interests, and that even horrifyingly immediate events, which cause unimaginable suffering to individuals, like the Vietnam and gulf wars, had become in some way just 'dramatized media events' which 'take place on TV' in scenes constructed for political ends by the cameras—the sniper with the camera over his shoulder, the speech-makers' hopes for the better on the White House lawn, and so on. (Butler, 110-11)

The **television codes** have been assigned three levels by Fiske, which are reality, representation and ideology. According to Fiske, the reality is the product of a given culture's codes. It means any event televised is actually encoded in social codes like dress, make-up, behaviour and speech. The second level, i.e. representation is through the technical apparatus like camera, lighting, music, etc. The third level of ideology makes sure that the representations of characters conforms to the ideological codes of patriarchy, class, race, capitalism, etc. It is these codes which finally decide the meanings of which society can make sense unless these are incoherent and incongruent. The seeming unity achieved through coherent meanings is prone to deconstruction.

Despite all this, however, Fiske does not subscribe to the widely prevalent pessimistic view that the television viewer is passive recipient of whatever is dished out to him on the idiot box. Instead, he believes that the viewer does to the TV screen what a reader does to the page of a book. "Programs are produced, distributed, and defined by the industry: texts are the product of their readers" (Fiske, 14). The meaning of a text comes out through negotiation between the text and the reader—a known phenomenological stand. In his opinion, the viewer can produce resistant reading and refuse to be taken in by the ideology of the TV programme.

It would appear that Fiske's views are relevant to an **enlightened audience** only. The mass of TV viewership is of average caliber. The gullibility is more pronounced in the case of poorly informed viewers spread over inaccessible terrains as is the situation in India. Add to this the recent phenomenon of 'sponsored news' about which the Press Council of India has been rightly concerned. But as it happens with 'surrogate advertising' for produces banned in advertising, the advertising industry, concerned as it is about its own profits, knows well how to circumvent the law and take in the gullible viewers ever ready to lap up whatever is dished out.

Under the circumstances, the attack on **advertising** for creating unnecessary consumption needs in society can be appreciated. The advertisements now focus on fashion or taste and image linked to a product and not on the utility aspect. Goods are promoted not because these are found to be useful but because one must keep up with the Joneses. Thus, a superficial consumerist culture is encouraged by the television. Kroker and Cook rightly point out that "In postmodernist culture, it's not TV as a mirror of society, but just the reverse: it's society as a mirror of television" (269). We can generalize this tendency on the basis of postmodern understanding of the linguistic notions of signifier/signified. It can be said that just as a signifier does not lead to the signified but being self-referential, leads to other signs, similarly the signs for objects do not lead to the desired object, rather these lead to other objects. The Indian notion of the insatiability of *vaasna* also conveys the same message.

The view that mass media has substituted **images for the real world** is linked at the root to the Marxist notion of 'false consciousness' which is supposed to have been brought about by the bourgeois discourse. This line of thinking also takes strength from the loss of faith in the realistic fiction of the 19th century. The poststructuralist thinking delinking signifier from the signified has only further fuelled the fire. There is, to be honest, the counter-view that questions, and even mocks the philosophical-structural notion when it comes to be applied to real life situation.

> So we never really get what we want anyway. But we might on the contrary say that we do indeed get what we pay for, however it is advertised—a McDonald hamburger is a McDonald's hamburger in all its billions of exemplifiers, and to many it really does taste pretty good. And if you smell of the Dune perfume you smell of Duneperfume. All this is not mere sign-play, [...] But to hear Baudrillard and others like him, you would think we ate, drank, and slept on and with mere signifiers. (Butler, 114)

The revolution seen in the development of microchip technology and advanced networking has influenced the human personality also and there have been any number of black prophecies made in this regard. One such is the envisioning of the world by robots. Films like *Terminator* (1984) in which the famous actor Schwarzenegger plays a cyborg killer, became a trend-setter. A recent Kamal Hassan starrer Indian film shows the robot developing human feelings of love! Likewise, the dissolution of human body and emergence of what has been called '**cyborg**'—a combination of cybernetics and human organism. The technology does not originate from the human body but enters the body. "Claims that the body has disappeared, that the body no longer exists, that the mind/body slit can be transcended, that the body is no longer 'human', all circulate in a number of debates about postmodernism" (Woods, 218). Similarly, the concept of 'body-without-organs' has been floated according to which the human body is so processed by the hyperereality that we experience our bodies only through the media imagery. Based upon these imaginings or insights, howsoever one might put it, the genre of cyberpunk fiction has made its entry into literature.

The conception of 'cyborg' has been hailed by the **feminists** as that would ensure the transcendence of gender, the social construction responsible for the woes of women all over the world! Such a body will also not to have the daily domestic grind to which a woman's body is subjected. Donna Haraway, the noted feminist, is particularly enthused about this possibility that betokens the effacement of gender hierarchies. In her book *Simians, Cyborgs and Women: The Reinvention of Nature* (1991), she avers that such a creature would be in a 'post-gender' world. "This cyborg becomes a symbol of the transgression of the boundaries between human and animal, organism and machine, the physical and the non-physical" (Woods, 221).

Apart from speculations about the emergence of 'cyborg', the cybernetic revolution has also focused attention on the notion of human **subjectivity** in this post-industrial information society. The new technologies define the prevailing notion of textuality afresh. Since subjectivity is a direct result of textual discourse prevailing at any point of time in society, the subjectivity or identity is bound to be redefined. Creating newer images of oneself on the net is a child's play. There are endless possibilities of the way one likes to be seen. There is no attachment to location now as the cyberspace is deterritorialised and there are no information barriers. Different types of people bring in different patterns of language use and thus create a new cyber milieu. It is indeed a global village, whose denizens can be called rootless nomads also. George Landow, in his *Hypertext: The Convergence of Contemporary Critical Theory and Technology* (1992), observes that in place of notions of centre, margin, hierarchy and linearity, we must re-inscribe those of nodes, multi-linearity and networks.

So, it is cybernetics, cyberspace and cyborgs that constitute the new-age discourse. The human body is in for change into a "techno-body, a screen, a hybridized version of pluralities: a cyborg, a hybrid, a body-without-organs, a virtual body, a body-in-process" (Woods, 220). All this boils down to what Baudrillard says about the reality of our times—**'hyperreality'**. In his "Simulacra and Simulations", his observation about society is: "As long as it was historically threatened by the real, power risked deterrence and simulation, disintegrating every contradiction by means of the reproduction of equivalent signs. When it is threatened today by simulation (the threat of vanishing in the play of signs), power risks the real, risks crisis, it gambles on remanufacturing artificial, social, economic, political stakes. This is a question of life or death for it. But it is too late" (409-10).

Works Cited

Baudrillard, Jean. "Simulacra and Simulations". *Modern Criticism and Theory: A Reader.* Eds. David Lodge & Nigel Wood. Essex: Pearson, 1988, Second Edition, 2000, pp. 403-12.

Butler, Christopher. *Postmodernism.* Oxford, UK: Oxford University Press, 2002.

Fiske, John. *Television and Society*. London: Methuen 1987, Reprint Routledge, 1999.

Hartley, John. *Key Concepts in Communication, Cultural and Media Studies.* Third Edition. London: Routledge, 2004.

Kroker, Arthur and David Cook. *The Postmodern Scene: Excremental Culture and Hyper-asesthetics.* Montreal: New World, 1988.

Woods, Tim. *Beginning Postmodernism.* New York: Manchester University Press, 1999.

29

Social Media Studies

By the term 'social media', we mean the websites like Facebook, Twitter, etc., which allow a platform to their users/ subscribers to interact through messages or exchange of visuals, etc. for personal or professional purpose. Social media, taken as a collective entity, also allows social networking and campaigning of different types about which sections of society are concerned. While the individuals use these sites mainly to promote friendships, business companies also use them to promote their businesses or to know about the personal life of their personnel. According to Nielsen, a global data organization, Internet users continue to spend more time with social media sites than any other site. The total time spent on social media in the U.S. across PC and mobile devices increased by 37 per cent to 121 billion minutes in July 2012 compared to 88 billion minutes in July 2011.

Tracing the **history** of social media, Miles Walker points out that social networking began in 1978 with the Bulletin Board System, which was "hosted on personal computers, requiring that users dial in through the modem of the host computer, exchanging information over phone lines with other users... it was quite slow since only one user could be logged in at a time." Geocities became the first social media site in 1994. Its initial purpose was to allow users to create their own websites, which were divided into 'cities', based on the website's content.

In 1995, TheGlobe.com was launched, offering users the ability to interact with people who held the same interests and publish their own content. Two years later, in 1997, AOL Instant Messenger and SixDegrees.com were launched. This was the year when instant messaging became popular and it was the first time Internet users were able to create a profile and befriend each other. Friendster was the pioneer of social networking. In its first three months, the social networking website acquired three million users. It served as the launching pad for the widely popular MySpace. In the following years, other social networking websites like Classmates.com, LinkedIn and Tribe. net started.

Facebook.com was launched in 2004 with the intent to connect U.S. college students, starting with Harvard College. Mark Zuckerberg, a sophomore at Harvard University, created an unofficial website 'thefacebook.com', the forerunner of the present Facebook, out of frustration that the university's official online Facebook project was taking too long. Social networking has come a long way since 1978 with Facebook having more than onebillion active users worldwide in October 2012. Recent figures suggest that Indian users of Net are double the number of American users and a substantial number is hooked to the social media sites. Social media technologies take on many different forms including magazines, Internet forums, weblogs, social blogs, social networks, podcasts, social bookmarking, voiceover IP, etc. There is an increasing trend towards using social media monitoring tools that allow marketers to search, track, and analyze conversation on the web about their brand or about topics of interest.

Kaplan and Haenlein created a **classification** scheme in their article *Business Horizons* (2010) with six different types of social media: collaborative projects like Wikipedia, blogging sites like Twitter, content communities like YouTube, networking sites like Facebook, virtual game sites like World of Warcraft, and virtual social world like Second Life. Several studies of the functioning and impact of social media on the lives of people have been carried out. Jan Kietzmann's Honeycomb Framework **theory** defines how social media services focus on some or all of seven functional building blocks. These explain the modes of the social media audiences. Thus, LinkedIn users are thought to care mostly about identity, reputation, and relationships; whereas YouTube's primary features are sharing, conversations, groups, and reputation. Many companies try to link these blocks to their brands by creating loyal communities. The function of public relations department of a company is to bolster such platforms. It also tackles any negative sentiments voiced at these forums because once these voices go viral, they can damage the company's reputation beyond repair.

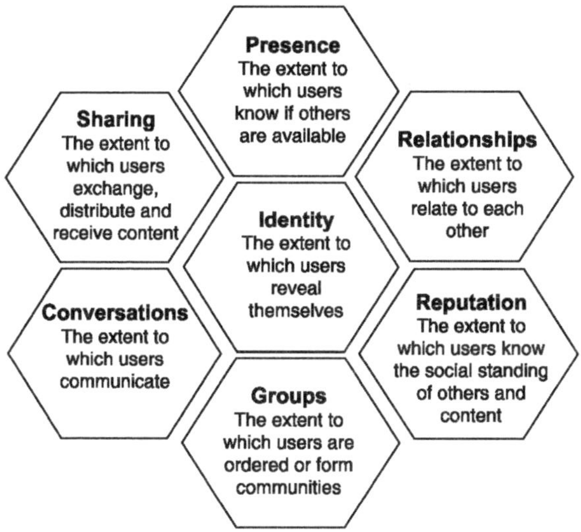

According to Jan H. Kietzmann, the Honeycomb framework of social media is based on the following functional building blocks:

1. Identity: It means that the users reveal their identities according to their choice. They may or may not reveal information like their name, age, sex, profession, location, etc.
2. Conversations: This block represents the limit of communication between different users of social media. People may write on wall, send message or blog to get in touch with like-minded people.

3. Sharing: Users of different social media platforms also like to share information, images, etc. when it suits their interests.
4. Presence: Some users are interested in knowing if others are accessible on the virtual platform. From there, they might like to get in touch in the real world also.
5. Relationships: The common denomination of relationship on social sites is 'friends', but this virtual friendship can grow into real friendship also.
6. Reputation: Users may also be interested in building up their reputation on the virtual platform.
7. Groups: The group functional block denotes the inclination of the users to form groups or communities based upon common interests.

In this way, social media makes an **impact** on the lives of the users and through the users on others in society. An increasing number of scholars have sought to study and measure the impact of social media. A 2010 study by the University of Maryland suggested that social media services might be addictive. Global consumers spend more than six hours on social networking sites. Several colleges and universities such as Harvard, Johns Hopkins, Columbia and Stanford among others, have introduced classes on best social media practices, preparing students for potential careers as digital strategists.

Various surveys reveal widespread social **media use** by individuals all over the world. It is interesting to note that people spend more time on social networks than on any other category of Internet site; it is roughly 20 per cent of their total time online spent through personal computer (PC), and 30 per cent of total time through mobile. Facebook remains the number one site which people visit; it is followed by Twitter. According to the statistics released by *Socialnomics* in June 2011, one out of eight couples married in the U.S. last year met via social media. Another survey reveals that one in five divorces also occurred due to Facebook.

The **positive effects** of social media and other Internet based social networks need not be over-emphasized. An interesting development has been the decline of journalistic influence as compared to that of the social networking sites like Facebook, YouTube and Twitter, which provide an alternative news source for users. All this not only upstages the conventional media such as press and television news but also itself plays a powerful role. Social media is used to forge friendships, exchange information, advertise products and services, launch collective action and undertake a hundred other actions. The Facebook communication played a big role in the uprising against the Egyptian regime in 2011. There are collective actions of non-political type also, like helping somebody or a large number of people in distress. In the aftermath of a natural calamity like the cloud-bursts and the consequent flash floods in Uttarakhand in June 2013 in which thousands of people perished, the social networking sites provided a very effective 'lost and found' platform. At times, literary groups have initiated joint writing of a long poem in which people situated far and wide have taken part and thus realized the ideal of oneness of mankind.

On the other hand, **negative aspects** of the burgeoning social media have been noted by several critics. They contend that the contents uploaded on the Twitter may have little relevance to the rest of the people who do not use Twitter. Some academics cast doubt on the openness and participatory character of the social media. A 'digital divide' has come into existence. This term (digital divide) was coined in 1996 by Lloyd Morrlsett to describe the gulf that purportedly separates information technology (IT) 'haves' from 'have-nots'. It is feared that the social media will increase an information disparity between winners, who are able to use the social media actively, and losers, who are not familiar with modern technologies. Moreover, social media content is generated through social media interactions done by the users through the site. The ownership and authenticity of the content on social media platforms has always generated controversy because the site though generated by the users is hosted by a company. Added to this is the danger to security of information, which can be leaked to third parties with economic interests in the platform, or parasites who comb the data for their own databases.

There has been much speculation about the meaningfulness of human interactions created by social media. It is widely believed that sites like Facebook discourage face-to-face interactions in society and actually make people lonely. A book by Sherry Turkle which has a fitting title—*Alone Together* (2011) —brings out the irony of situation in which we demand more from technology and less from one another. The negative use of social media for cyber bullying, sexual offences and cheating has also come to light. Parents are worried about children exploring sites which promote sex, drugs, etc. According to some medical experts, social media addiction can be regarded as a real medical condition. Thus, the emergence and spread of social media sites on the net has been a mixed blessing for the contemporary man. If used with caution, it can be a boon but if indulged in recklessly, it turns soon into a bane.

Works Cited

H. Kietzmann, Jan; Kristopher Hermkens 'Social media? Get serious! Understanding the functional building blocks of social media'. *Business Horizons* 54 (2010): 241-51.

Kaplan Andreas M., Haenlein Michael (2010). 'Users of the world, unite! The challenges and opportunities of social media'. *Business Horizons* 53.1 (2010): 61.

Nielsen. "State of the media: The social media report 2012". 12 April 2012. Accessed 30 August 2013.<http://www.nielsen.com/us/en/reports/2012/state-of-the-media-the-social-media-report-2012.html>

Turkle, S. *Alone together*. New York: Basic Books, 2012.

Walker, Miles. 'The History of Social Networking.' *Webmaster View*. Accessed 14 August 2013. <http://www.webmasterview.com/2011/08/social-networking-history>

Bibliography

Abrams, M.H. and Geoffrey Gait Harpham. *A Handbook of Literary Terms*. New Delhi: Cengage Learning, 2009.

Ashcrolt, Bill et al. *Key Concepts in Post-colonial Studies*. London: Routledge. Indian Reprint.

Barry, Peter. *Beginning Theory: An Introduction to Literary and Cultural Theory*. Manchester, UK: Manchester University Press, 1999.

Batra, Jagdish. *T.S. Eliot: A Deconstructive Reading*. New Delhi: Prestige, 2010.

———, ed. *Form and Style in Indian English Fiction*. New Delhi: Prestige, 2011.

Bertens, Hans. *Literary Theory: The Basics*. Oxford: Routledge. 2001.

Bhabha, Homi K. *The Location of Culture*. London: Routledge. 1994.

Bhabha, Homi K., ed. *Nation and Narration*. London: Routledge, 1990.

Blackbury, Malcolm. *The Social Context of Modern English Literature*. Oxford: Basil Blackwell, 1971.

Butler, Christopher. *Postmodernism*. Oxford. UK: Oxford University Press, 2002.

Chaudhuri, Maitrayee, ed. *Feminism in India*. 2004. New Delhi: Kali for Women & Women unlimited, 2006.

Collingwood, R.G. *The Idea of History* (Revised Edition). New Delhi: Oxford, 2004. Sixth Impression 2010.

Cuddon, J.A. *A Dictionary of Literary Terms and Literary Theory* (Fourth Edition). New Delhi: Maya Blackwell. 1998.

Culler, Jonathan. *Structuralist Poetics*. London: Routledge, 1975. Indian reprint, 2012.

Culler, Jonathan. *The Pursuit of Signs: Semiotics, Literature, Deconstruction*. London: Routledge, 2001.

Day, Gary, *Literary Criticism: A New History*. Edinburgh: Edinburgh University Press Ltd., 2008, Paperback Edition 2010.

Eagleton, Terry. *Literary Theory: An Introduction*. Second Edition. New Delhi: Maya Blackwell, 2000.

Ecocriticism Reader: Landmarks in Literary Ecology. Eds. Cheryll Glotfelty and Harold Iromni. Athens and London: The University of Georgia Press, 1996.

Fanon, Franz. *The Wretched of the Earth*. London: Penguin, 1967. Reprint, 1990.

Forster, E.M. *Aspects of the Novel*. Harmondsworth, U.K.: Penguin, 1962.

Frye, Northrop. *The Stubborn Critic: Essays on Criticism and Society*, 1970. Oxen: Routledge, 2011.

Ghosh, Arpita. 'Indian Feminism: A Debate on the incorporation of the "alien" culture within the "native" tradition.' Muse India. Issue 50: July-Aug. 2013. http://museindia.com/regularcontent.asp?issid=34&id=2311>

Guerin, Wilfred L. et al. *A Handbook of Critical Approaches to Literature*, fifth edition. New Delhi: Oxford University Press, 2006.

Habib, M.A.R. *A History of Literary Criticism*. Oxford: Blackwell Publishing. 2005. Indian Reprint, 2006.

———. *Modern Literary Criticism and Theory: A History*. Oxford: Blackwell, 2008. Reprint, 2013.

Hartley, John. *Key Concepts in Communication, Cultural and Media Studies*. Third Edition. London: Routledge, 2004.

Holy Bible. King James Version. Madras: India Bible Literature, 1980.

Husserl, Edmund. 'Pure Phenomenology, Its Method and Its Field of Investigation' Inaugural Lecture at Freiburg imBreisgau, 3 May 1917, tr. Robert Welsh Jordan.http://lamar.colostate.edu/~rwjordan/W-INAUGFRB.HTML

Hutcheon, Linda. *A Theory of Parody: The Teachings of Twentieth-Century Art Forms*. New York: Methuen, 1985.

Indian Journal of Ecocriticism. OSLE India. Vol. 2, Aug. 2000.

Indigo Dictionary of Philosophy. New Delhi: Cosmo, 2002.

John Hopkins Guide to Literary Theory & Criticism. Second Edition. Eds. Groden, Michael et al. Baltimore: The John Hopkins University Press, 2005.

Jain, Jasbir. *Writing Women Across Cultures*. Jaipur and New Delhi: Rawat Publications, 2002.

———. *Indigenous Roots of Feminism: Culture, Subjectivity and Agency*. New Delhi: Sage, 2011.

Jefferson, Ann and David Robey, eds. *Modern Literary Theory: A Comparative Introduction*. Batsford, 1986.

Jenni, Ramone. *Postcolonial Theories*. London: Palgrave Mamillan, 2011.

Kellogg, Robert el al: *The Nature of Narrative*. New York: Oxford, 2006.

Kumar, Radha. *The History of Doing: An Illustrated Account of Movements for Women's Rights and Feminism in India, 1800-1990*. New Delhi: Zubaan-Kali for Women, 2009.

Nabar, Vrinda. *Caste As Woman*. New Delhi: Penguin Books. India, 1995.

Lecch, Geoffrey N. and Michael H. Short. *Style in Fiction*. London: Longman. 1981. Fourth reprint, 1985.

Lodge, David and Nigel Wood, eds. *Modern Criticism and Theory: A Reader*. Essex: Pearson. 1988. Second edition, 2000.

Malik, R.S. *English for UGC-NET/JRF/SLET*. New Delhi: Atlantic, 2013.

Mitra Ananda. 'Characteristics of the WWW Text: Tracing Discursive Strategies". *Journal of Computer Mediated Communication*, 1999:5(1): 1.

Modern Criticism and Theoiy: A Reader. Eds. Lodge David and Nigel Wood Essex: Pearson, 1988. Second edition, 2000.

Mohanty, Chandra Talpade. 'Under Western Eyes: Feminist Scholarship and Colonial Discourses.' *Feminist Review*, No. 30 (1988): 61-88. JSTOR 10 July 2013. <http://www.jslor.org/stable/1395054>

Nandan, Satendra, 'Diasporic Consciousness.' *Interrogating Post-colonial Theory, Text and Context*. Ed. Harish Trivedi and Meenakshi Mukherjee. Shimla: Indian Institute of Advanced Studies, 1996.

Nayar, Pramod. *Contemporary Literary and Cultural Theory: From Structuralism to Ecocriticism*. New Delhi: Longman. 2011.

Rimmon-Kenan, Shlomilh. *Narrative Fiction*. London: Routledge. 1983. Edition, 2005.

Roberts, Adam. *Fredric Jameson*. London: Routledge, 2007.

Rushdie, Salman. *Imaginary Homelands*. London: Granta Books, 1992.

Ryan, Michael. *Literary Theory: A Practical Introduction*. New York: Blackwell, 1999. Indian Reprint, 2002.

Said, Edward. *Culture and Imperialism*. London: Chatto & Windus, 1993.

Selden, Raman. *A Reader's Guide to Contemporary Literary Theory*. Sussex: Harvester, 1985.

Sharma, J.C. Inaugural Address. "Indian diaspora: Responsibilities and Relationships, Strengths, Weaknesses and Contribution." *Theorizing and Critiquing Indian Diaspora*, Ed. Adesh Pal. New Delhi: Creative, 2004.

Spivak, Gayatri Chakravorty. *In Other Worlds*. New York: Methuen 1987. Routledge, 2006. Reprint, 2012.

Sturrock, John. *Structuralism*. (Second edition). Oxford. UK: Blackwell, 2003.

Waugh, Patricia, ed. *Literary Theory and Criticism*. Oxford: Oxford University Press. 2006, Third Impression, 2009.

Wales, Katie. *A Dictioary of Stylistics*. Essex: Pearson, 2001.

Watts, Alan W. *Myth and Ritual in Christianity*. New York: Beacon, 1954.

Webster, Roger. *Studying Literary Theory: An Introduction* (Second Edition). London: Hodder Headline, 1996. Reprint, 2001.

Woods, Tim. *Beginning Postmodernism*. New York: Manchester University Press, 1999.